Berlitz®

Australia

Text Ken Bernstein
Revised by Peter Needham
Editor Jeffery Pike
Principal Photography Jon Davison;
Australian Tourist Commission
Cover Photograph Australian
Tourist Commission
Cartography Maria Randell
Design Klaus Geisler
Managing Editor Tony Halliday

NEXT
6 km

Berlitz POCKET GUIDE

Australia

Eleventh edition 2003 (Reprinted 2004)

PHOTOGRAPHY CREDITS

All photographs are by Jon Davison or supplied by the Australian Tourist Commission except those on pages 14, 126, 131, 133, 135, 136, 193, 219 by Glyn Genin; 11, 76, 97, 109, 210, 222, 223 by Kevin Hamdorf; 31, 43, 92, 95, 105, 113, 114, 117, 140, 161, 201 by Claude Hüber; 172, 174 by Peter Lalor; 16 by P&O Australia Resort; 40 by Tony Perrottet; 10, 80, 81, 85, 86, 90, 100, 146, 217 by Steven Pohlner; 89 by Quicksilver Connections; 177, 178 by Sovereign Hill Museums Association; 30, 164, 167, 168, 171 by Andrew Tauber.

CONTACTING THE EDITORS

Every effort has been made to provide accurate information in this publication, but changes are inevitable. The publisher cannot be responsible for any resulting loss, inconvenience or injury. We would appreciate it if readers would call our attention to any errors or outdated information by contacting Berlitz Publishing, PO Box 7910, London SE1 1WE, England. Fax: (44) 20 7403 0290; email: berlitz@apaguide.co.uk www.berlitzpublishing.com

© 2004 Apa Publications GmbH & Co. Verlag KG, Singapore Branch, Singapore

Maps © 2004 Apa Publications GmbH & Co. Verlag KG, Singapore Branch, Singapore

Printed in Singapore by Insight Print Services (Pte) Ltd, 38 Joo Koon Road, Singapore 628990.
Tel : (65) 6865-1600. Fax : (65) 6861-6438

Berlitz Trademark Reg. U.S. Patent Office and other countries. Marca Registrada. Used under licence from the Berlitz Investment Corporation

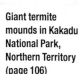

Giant termite mounds in Kakadu National Park, Northern Territory (page 106)

The Blue Mountains (page 61), west of Sydney, defied the first colonists for many years

The Great Ocean Road (page 179) offers views of spectacular rock formations

The Great Barrier Reef, off Queensland's coast (page 87), is one of the natural wonders of the world

TOP TEN ATTRACTIONS

Unique to Australia, kangaroos (page 156) come in many shapes and sizes

Perth (page 125) is a stylish and vibrant modern city

Elegant Melbourne (page 161), a sophisticated modern city

Barossa Valley in South Australia (page 152) is the most attractive wine-growing region

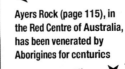

Ayers Rock (page 115), in the Red Centre of Australia, has been venerated by Aborigines for centuries

The Sydney Opera House, (page 53) is a unique icon of Australia

CONTENTS

Fact Sheets

INTRODUCTION

Australia bounded into the 21st century with great optimistic exuberance, spurred on by the sensational Sydney 2000 Olympic Games. 'I invite you to suggest a more successful event anywhere in the peacetime history of mankind,' effused US travel writer Bill Bryson, in the London *Times*.

The Games focused unprecedented media attention on the Land Down Under, a country that in many people's minds had always consisted of vague images: the Sydney Opera House, the Great Barrier Reef, the unforgiving Outback, and all those cute and bizarre Australian animals. It's true that the kangaroo, the koala, the wombat, the duck-billed platypus and the

> In 1922 D.H. Lawrence wrote: 'Australia is like an open door with the blue beyond. You just walk out of the world and into Australia.'

Tasmanian devil exist nowhere else in the world outside zoos – and neither does anything resembling them. There is, of course, much more to the country than this.

Media coverage of the Olympics helped broaden Australia's image and move it away from the 'reef, desert, koalas and crocs' stereotype. The Games became the most-watched event in history, with more than 3.8 billion people worldwide tuning in. Between the sporting contests, viewers caught glimpses of Australia's people, beaches, cityscapes and architecture. They liked what they saw.

Although the Games belonged to Sydney, Australia's largest city, the benefits flowed widely across the entire country. A record 4.9 million international tourists visited

A lifeguard surveys the South Bank beach, Brisbane

Australia in 2000 – 11 percent more than in 1999. The tourist boom shows no sign of slowing in the coming years; visitor arrivals are forecast to increase annually to 10 million by 2010, a figure equal to about half of Australia's population. In January 2001, the premiere episode of *Survivor II, The Australian Outback* was watched by 42 million US television viewers. That, and the programme's subsequent episodes, spurred even more interest in the great southern island continent.

It all represents a massive turnaround for a country that, for most of its history, has been little known and even less understood. A character in an Oscar Wilde play set in Queen Victoria's heyday summed up the foreigner's blurred impression of Australia: 'It must be so pretty with all the dear little kangaroos flying about. Agatha has found it on the map.'

Aussie Stereotypes

Similarly fuzzy impressions persisted for decades. Australia is still perceived as a quirky, topsy-turvy land shared by eccentric marsupials and a laid-back human population that is fond of sunbathing, surfing and swilling cold beer.

Like most clichés, there's something to it. Most Aussies (pronounced 'ozzies') relish the outdoor life. Many radiate health and either possess or admire tanned muscles. If they're not actually at the beach, male Aussies are likely to be hiking, jogging, playing football (or at least listening to football or cricket on the radio), or they are out in the garden barbecuing beef or seafood. To complete the picture, there's usually an icy beer at hand to pacify the fiercest thirst. Australians may not be the world's most insatiable beer drinkers, but they're high in the league.

Prospectors seeking gold, opals or other minerals still roam the stark Outback. In Australia's wild northern 'Top End', enormous crocodiles and deadly snakes stalk unwary

There are ten times as many sheep as people in Australia

prey – including occasional human victims. Remote cattle farms are so big that cowboys conduct their roundups using helicopters. One of the ranches is the size of Belgium.

However, these startling facts represent only part of the truth. Camping vacations are as close as the overwhelming majority of Australians get to living in the bush. Australia is one of the world's most urbanised countries, with over 90 percent of its population living near the coast in the 10 biggest cities. More than one Australian in five resides in Sydney (population 4 million). Melbourne is approaching the same size. Other state capitals – Brisbane, Adelaide and Perth – account for most of the rest of the population.

For many people, Australia's natural wonders, its odd wildlife and its far-flung open spaces still eclipse everything else. The vast and eerily beautiful Outback holds an almost hypnotic appeal. When best-selling thriller author Stephen King took a short break from writing in 1997 and roared into

**Marsupial mammals
dominate Australia's fauna**

Australia's great wide-open expanses on a motorcycle, he described his sense of awe: 'If you stop, the silence is incredible. You feel very small; you can almost hear God breathing.'

Extraordinary wildlife wanders the Outback. Australia has a virtual monopoly on monotremes, the generic name for a type of mammal that includes the waddling, spine-covered echidna and the platypus, an egg-laying furry mammal with a duck-like beak.

Rather more familiar are Australia's marsupials, equipped with pouches to solve the baby-sitting problem. Bounding across the Australian landscape are numerous varieties of mocropods ('big feet'), from small wallabies to giant red kangaroos big enough to cow any heavyweight boxer. Another marsupial, the languid, furry koala, eschews violent exercise, spending its days drowsing in the branches in a eucalyptus-induced haze. Its relative, the wombat – another vegetarian marsupial – prefers to burrow under stumps or logs, or in the banks of creeks.

Birdwatchers here can count hundreds of species. Thrillingly colourful birds are as common as sparrows, and lyrical or humorous birdcalls provide every evening's country music. These indigenous stars have names such as flowerpecker, honeyeater and kookaburra, but the favourite bird of crossword puzzlers – the emu – can't sing or fly.

Unsurprisingly, Australia has some unique specialities in the reptile department, too, including 2-m (6-ft) goannas, exotic creatures like the frill-necked lizard and the bearded dragon, and the world's largest crocodile, the salt-water croc, or 'saltie'. For good measure, the island contains more species of venomous snake than anywhere else on earth.

A Continent Cut Off

Australia has been isolated from other continents since it split from the remnants of the southern super-continent, Gondwana, about 40 million years ago. Cut off from the evolutionary mainstream, plants and animals developed in ways that have engrossed generations of scientists and astounded thousands of ordinary tourists.

For countless millennia, the only humans sharing the continent with these native animals were nomadic Aboriginal tribes. These first Australians are believed to have arrived from Asia, probably by boat, somewhere between 50,000 and 100,000 years ago – possibly even further back. Australia's Aborigines lived within tribal boundaries they believed had been created by hero ancestors in a period called the Dreamtime. Aborigines built no permanent structures but lived in a manner that ensured their survival in a harsh environment.

Their lives changed little until European explorers

Captain Cook claimed territory in the name of King George III

began arriving in the 17th and 18th centuries. The colonial history of Australia began in 1770 when renowned English navigator Captain James Cook landed on Australia's east coast and claimed all the territory he charted for King George III. Shortly after Cook's arrival, the British decided Australia was an ideal place to send convicts and in 1787, Britain dispatched a fleet of soldiers and convicts to colonise Australia, one of the farthest-flung points of its Empire.

> **In Australia, four out of 10 of the population are immigrants or the first-generation children of immigrants.**

In a relatively short time, the British Empire had casually seized the traditional lands of Australia's dark-skinned hunter-gatherers. Aborigines were dispersed and massacred. Australia's indigenous people (who now represent about one percent of the country's population) did not gain the vote until 1962 and were not included in Australia's official census until 1967.

The fact that modern Australia can be traced back to chain gangs of convicted felons rather than to resolute idealists has left its mark on the national psyche, although the impact is fading. Australians were once notably defensive about their country, asking foreigners what they thought of it, then waiting anxiously for the answer. These days, Aussies are more relaxed about such matters. The descendants of convicts have long since been outnumbered by the descendants of free settlers, but if Australians can prove convict ancestry they do so eagerly – it's considered a mark of prestige.

The country has much to be proud of. In little more than 200 years, a tiny European settlement founded in conditions of brutality, servitude and privation has prospered and transformed itself into a dynamic modern nation whose economy places it in the top 10 OECD countries in terms of gross domestic product. Tourism is the largest earner of foreign exchange and a major employer, accounting for 500,000 jobs directly, or almost seven percent of Australia's workforce.

Australia is a long way from northern-hemisphere population centres: 9,720km (6,000 miles) from the USA, 17,820km (11,000 miles) from Britain. But non-stop or one-stop flights make the going relatively easy. More distant in cultural terms are Australia's nearest neighbours, Indonesia and Papua New Guinea, a kangaroo's hop to the north. The Asian connection is becoming more important, not only politically and economically, but in human terms; a look at the faces on any city street shows the vastly increased flow of immigrants from Southeast Asia.

Since the early 1990s, cultural intermingling has revolutionised the national diet. Urban Australia now enjoys a collage of culinary influences on fresh, high-quality ingredients. All the state capitals have lively café scenes and at least

Beware of wildlife – including wild camels

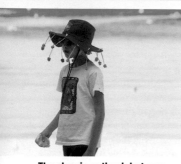

The classic outback hat was designed to keep flies away

one wine-growing area nearby, giving the chance to sample wines at the cellar door. Climatic diversity allows Australia to produce warm- and cool-climate wines and grow exotica such as rambutans, custard apples, mangoes, bok choy, mizuna and lychees, as well as more familiar apples, strawberries, blackberries, coconuts and mandarins.

In big cities, including Sydney, Melbourne or Brisbane, you'll have no trouble finding restaurants serving excellently prepared cuisine from as far afield as Thailand, Mexico, Cambodia, Japan, France, Hungary, Spain, Lebanon, Turkey or Italy. In smaller towns, the choice is more limited, and you may have to settle for a meat pie, fish and chips or chop suey.

Australia's geographical superlatives are clear-cut. It is the world's biggest island. More accurately, it is the smallest and least populous (about 19 million inhabitants) of the continents, and the only one housing a single nation. Australia measures about 4,000km (2,500 miles) east to west and 3,200km (2,000 miles) north to south. It occupies approximately the same area as the 48 contiguous states of the USA, or about 24 times the area of the British Isles.

The Great Dividing Range, stretching almost the entire length of the eastern continent, separates a narrow fertile strip on the coast from the Outback. West of the range, the country becomes increasingly flat and dry. Habitation eventually ceases and – after thousands of miles – the horizon is broken only by occasional mysterious protuberances including Ayers

Rock and the Olgas, and starkly beautiful mountains such as the Flinders and Macdonnell ranges. Then, in the far south of Western Australia, a repeat of the mountain range-coastal strip pattern heralds the Indian Ocean.

While Outback Australia includes regions of breathtaking natural beauty, much of the interior is arid, consisting of immense deserts and salt pans. Only nine percent of the country is arable, which is why the settlement pattern has been so different from that of the USA, and why the population is so much smaller. Non-arable land is not necessarily unproductive: under the surface lie bauxite, coal, iron ore, copper, tin, silver, uranium, nickel, tungsten, lead, zinc, diamonds, natural gas and oil.

A Variety of Vegetation

Australia is home to some of the world's best-preserved wilderness areas. The World Heritage List currently includes 13 Australian regions, ranging from the Great Barrier Reef and the Tasmanian Wilderness to the Wet Tropics of Queensland and the Blue Mountains, the latter a day-trip from Sydney.

Australia's rainforests, healthy, vast and diverse, form one of the world's best-preserved wilderness resources. From the lush, dense jungles of Tropical North Queensland, the rainforest region extends south to the planet's last great stand of temperate rainforest – the cool, moist forests of Tasmania. Apart from their sheer beauty, Australia's

Australia has unique and bizarre plants as well as animals

rainforests contain about half of all Australian plant species, including 'primitive' plant families providing direct links with the birth of flowering plants over 100 million years ago.

At almost all Australian latitudes you'll see hardy trees of two main families. There are more than 600 species of flowering acacia (including the golden wattle from which Australia derives its national colours) and over 500 types of eucalyptus, ranging from low, stunted, scrub-like bushes to the great towering varieties of the highland forests. There are ghost gums, so-called because under the light of the moon they appear silvery-white, and rock-hard ironbarks, capable of blunting the toughest timber saws.

Australia is the world's flattest continent, although the nation's summit, Mt Kosciuszko (elevation 2,228m/7,308ft), is almost as high as Mexico City. You can ski in the Snowy Mountains in August. The country's first ski club, the

The Great Barrier Reef is the world's largest living organism

Kiandra Snow-Shoe Club, was founded in 1870 – two years before the first clubs in the United States.

Australia is the driest continent, with only one river (the Murray) worthy of world ranking. The country's coastline of 36,735km (almost 23,000 miles) includes many sweeping empty beaches where you can see nobody for a whole day or longer. You can dip a toe, or a surfboard, in legendary seas and oceans, among them the Coral Sea, the Timor Sea, the Indian Ocean and the Southern Ocean.

> **The Great Barrier Reef is home to more than 1,000 species of fish as well as whales, dolphins, turtles and thousands of different crustaceans.**

Underwater Wonders

Some of Australia's most colourful sights exist under the sea. Divers visit Australian waters to admire the sort of fish you see in a collector's tropical tank – only 10 times bigger. Gorgeous angel fish and moorish idols glide past the enthralled skin diver's mask. Big-mouthed sharks and venomous scorpion fish may also be seen.

For enthusiasts of underwater spectacles, the most exciting place in the world is the Great Barrier Reef. This 1,944-km- (1,200-mile-) long miracle – a living structure of coral – thrills the imagination in its immensity and in the intricate detail of brightly hued organisms shaped like antlers, flowers, fans or brains. It's the world's largest living thing. The most sublime tropical fish congregate here, too.

The reef, one of Australia's top tourist destinations, has become ever more accessible. So has Ayers Rock, complete with its own airport and hotel complex. Australia's highly developed transport system puts the whole continent within reach: beaches and ski resorts, dynamic cities and Outback ghost towns.

Even among such a wealth of natural wonders, it's the people you meet who often leave the deepest impression.

Australians generally are a friendly, no-nonsense bunch – direct and to the point. 'Gidday mate!' is a cheery greeting used often, sometimes followed by 'How ya goin', alright?' Americans detect Cockney or Irish overtones in the Australian accent – yet some visitors from Britain or Ireland swear they can identify an American influence.

Many Australian terms are unique, as likely to baffle a Brit or American as a European. 'Don't come the raw prawn' is a picturesque example, fading now from general usage. It means 'Don't try to pull the wool over my eyes.' The happy-go-lucky expression 'She'll be right' has been largely supplanted by 'No worries, mate,' but they both mean the same thing – 'It will all be ok.'

The Aussie sense of humour can bewilder newcomers. It is peppered with ironic understatements and playful contradictions, such as: 'She's getting a bit warm' (as the shade temperature reaches 40°C or 104°F); 'You're not wrong,

The Commonwealth of Australia

Since 1901 the six former British colonies of Australia have been an independent federal commonwealth with a British-style parliamentary system. The Head of State is the Governor-General, nominated by the federal government and appointed by the Queen. There is a three-tiered system of government: federal, state and local. The Prime Minister heads the federal government and is the leader of the party that holds the most seats in the lower chamber, the House of Representatives. The upper house is the Senate. The federal parliament is based in Canberra, a city founded in 1927 to prevent the rival cities of Sydney and Melbourne battling for the honour of being the nation's capital. Like Washington DC, in the USA, Canberra lies in its own administrative zone, the Australian Capital Territory (ATC). Each state has its own government and premier.

'mate' (an expression of enthusiastic agreement); or 'Now there's a bloke who hates a drink' (meaning that the man is a heavy drinker).

Until recently, Australia was a man's world, where the missus stayed at home scrubbing the floor while the husband played football with his mates, talked macho and drank a lot. Early in the 20th century, the popular Australian poet, Henry

A kangaroo and emu support Australia's coat of arms

Lawson, explained this drinking as 'a man's way of crying'. The gender gulf appears to have narrowed, particularly in urban Australia, and a woman's place is now on par with her sisters in other industrialised western societies.

Australia's cultural mix is still evolving, with Britain and the USA as the main influences. British visitors notice a California-style informality; American visitors are often surprised by the degree of Britishness remaining. At leisure, the majority of young Australians dress like Americans and watch much the same TV shows, but students at private schools continue to wear blazers and straw boaters like their counterparts in England. Cricket is played on local greens and lawyers appear in court in British-style gowns and horsehair wigs.

Uniting Aussies of all classes, origins and persuasions are a love of outdoor enjoyment, a passion for sport and a zest for gambling, on anything from horse races to one-armed bandits (poker machines or 'pokies'). These three pursuits have delighted the citizenry ever since modern Australia was founded.

A BRIEF HISTORY

Australia may have been populated for longer than Western Europe – possibly twice as long. Experts are divided about the dates, with some scientists suggesting that the first inhabitants of Australia arrived 40,000 or 50,000 years ago, others arguing that it was far earlier. Dr Paul Tacon, head of the People and Place Research Centre of the Australian Museum, says that pollen core samples taken across Australia show changes in vegetation and deposition of charcoal 'beginning somewhere about 120,000 years ago'. He believes that these changes probably resulted from human activity.

The first migrations to Australia were most likely spurred by a period of glacial advance that encouraged the shivering cave-dwellers of the Northern Hemisphere to head for the sun belt. This move set off a chain reaction, forcing more southerly folk out of their way. As ice caps accumulated, sea levels dropped drastically. So, in a search for greener pastures or more elbow-room, or perhaps blown off course, the original immigrants arrived Down Under by boat from the north.

Ancient Aboriginal rock art

The first Australians had little difficulty adapting to the new environment. As Stone Age hunter-gatherers, they were accustomed to foraging, and the takings in the new continent were good: plenty of fish, berries and roots and, for a change of diet, why not go out and spear a kangaroo?

'The Dreamtime' is the all-purpose name for everything that came before. It puts Aboriginal history, traditions and culture under a single mythological roof. The Dreamtime's version of Genesis recounts how ancestral heroes created the stars, the earth and all the creatures. The Dreamtime explains why the animals and plants are the way they are, and how humans can live in harmony with nature.

Stone Age paintings reveal a developed aesthetic sense

Navigators Arrive

For many millennia the Aborigines had Australia to themselves. But over the last few hundred years, the rest of the world began closing in. Like the search for El Dorado, everybody seemed to be looking for *Terra Australis Incognita*, the 'Unknown Land of the South'. Throughout the 16th century, explorers from Europe kept their eyes peeled for the legendary continent and its presumed riches. Some (including the Spanish, Portuguese and Chinese) may have come close, but the first known landing was by a Dutch captain, Willem Jansz, in 1606. It was something of an anticlimax. 'There was no good to be done there,' was Jansz's conclusion as he weighed anchor.

However, the merchant adventurers of the Dutch East India Company were not to be discouraged. In 1642 the company dispatched one of its ace seafarers, Abel Tasman, to track down the elusive treasures of the farthest continent. On his first expedition, Tasman discovered an island that he called Van Diemen's Land – now known as Tasmania, after him. A couple of years later he was sent back. He covered much of the coast of northern Australia, but still found no gold, silver or spices. Like Jansz before him, Tasman had nothing good to say about the indigenous people, who impressed him as poor, hungry and unattractive brutes. The Dutch named Australia New Holland, but their reports on the land were so unpromising that they never bothered to claim it.

Another pessimistic view was reported by a colourful traveller, English buccaneer William Dampier, who had two good looks at the west coast of Australia towards the end of the 17th century. He found no drinking water, no fruit or vegetables, no riches and 'the miserablest people in the world'.

Botany Bay

Almost by accident, Captain James Cook, the great British navigator, landed on the east coast of Australia in 1770 on a very roundabout trip back to England from Tahiti. Aboard his ship *Endeavour* were the skilled naturalists Joseph Banks and Daniel Solander. They found so many fascinating specimens that Cook was moved to name the place Botany Bay.

Cook claimed all the territory he charted for George III, coining the name New South Wales. He returned to London with glowing reports of the Australia he had seen: a vast, sunny, fertile land, inhabited by a native people who were 'far more happier than we Europeans'.

In 1779, Joseph Banks, by now the president of the Royal Society, came up with a novel idea. He formally proposed colonising Australia, but instead of conventional settlers, he would send out convicts as pioneers.

> **According to the author Mark Twain, the history of Australia 'does not read like history but like the most beautiful lies... It is full of surprises, and adventures, and incongruities, and contradictions, and incredibilities; but they are all true; they all happened.'**

This plan, he contended, would solve the crisis in Britain's overflowing jails.

For most of the 18th century, the British had disposed of troublesome convicts by banishing them to North America. With the American Revolution, though, this destination had to be dropped from the itineraries. The motherland's prisons could not cope, and the river hulks that were used as floating jails threatened riot and disease.

Banks's proposal for a prison island on the other side of the globe seemed far-fetched and expensive, but, with no alternatives, in May 1787 the British government

Cook's *Endeavour*, a converted collier, rides a South Pacific storm

began the transportation of criminals to Australia. The programme was to endure for 80 years. In that time more than 160,000 convicts were shipped to a new life Down Under.

The First Fleet

A retired naval officer, Captain Arthur Phillip, was put in command of the first fleet of 11 sailing vessels carrying nearly 1,500 people – more than half of them convicts – on an eight-month voyage from Portsmouth to New South Wales. Against the odds, the convoy was a success.

Captain Phillip (now titled Governor) came ashore in full ceremonial dress but unarmed. Spear-toting natives milled about like an unwelcoming committee. A lieutenant on the flagship wrote: 'I think it is very easy to conceive the ridiculous figure we must appear to these poor creatures, who were perfectly naked.' It also unveiled the truth about Botany Bay: Captain Cook's rosy claims faded to bleak. The expedition's officers were appalled to discover that there was no shelter from east winds, that much of the alleged meadowland was actually swamp and that there was not enough fresh water to go around.

Luckily, the next best thing to paradise was waiting just around the corner. Governor Phillip, together with a reconnaissance party, sailed 20km (12 miles) up the coast and discovered what Fleet Surgeon John White modestly called 'the finest and most extensive harbour in the universe'. It could, he determined provide 'safe anchorage for all the navies of Europe'. It was also strikingly beautiful. Today it is decorated with an Opera House and a bridge and is called Sydney Harbour. The fleet reassembled at Sydney Cove on 26 January 1788 (the date is marked every year as the Australian national holiday), and the British flag was raised over the brand-new colony.

London's great expectations took for granted that

Captain James Cook, as portrayed by Nathaniel Dance

New South Wales would be instantly self-sufficient. Real life fell dangerously short of the theory. The Sydney summer was too hot for exertion, and even if the convicts had genuinely wanted to pitch in, the soil was unpromising. In any event, most of the outcasts were city-bred and didn't know the difference between a hoe and a sickle. Livestock died or disappeared in the bush.

Shipwrecks and delays in London meant that relief supplies were delayed for nearly two years of increasing desperation. As food supplies dwindled, rations were cut. Prisoners caught stealing food were flogged. Finally, to set an example, the Governor ordered a food looter to be hanged.

In June 1790, to all-round jubilation, the supply ship *Lady Juliana* reached Sydney harbour and the long fast ended. As agriculture finally began to blossom, many thousands of new prisoners were shipped out. And even voluntary settlers chose Australia as the land of their future.

Enter Captain Bligh

When Governor Phillip retired, the colony's top army officer, Major Francis Grose, took over. His army subordinates fared very well under the new regime, which encouraged free enterprise. The officers soon found profitable sidelines, usually at the expense of the British taxpayers. The army's monopoly on the sale of rum made quick fortunes; under some tipsy economic law, rum began to replace money as Australia's medium of exchange. Even prisoners were paid in alcohol for their extracurricular jobs.

As news of widespread hanky-panky reached London, the government responded by sending out a well-known disciplinarian to shake up the rum-sodden militia. He was Captain William Bligh, target of the notorious mutiny on *HMS Bounty* seven years earlier. Bligh meant to put fear into the hearts of backsliding officers, but his explosive temper was beyond control. His New South Wales victims nicknamed the new governor Caligula and plotted treason.

Bligh was deposed by a group of insurgent officers on 26 January 1808, as the colony toasted its 20th anniversary. The Rum Rebellion, as the mutiny was dubbed, led to a radical reorganisation and reshuffle in personnel. But the inevitable court-martial seemed to understand how Bligh's personality and methods had galled his subordinates. The mutineers were finally punished by more than a rap on the knuckles, but less than they might have expected.

Opening a Continent

New South Wales, under Governor Lachlan Macquarie, overcame the stigma of a penal colony and became a land of opportunity. The idealistic army officer organised the building of schools, a hospital and a courthouse, and roads to link them. As a method of inspiration for exiles to go straight and win emancipation, Macquarie appointed an ex-convict as

Brave but Fallible

Captain William Bligh would not have won any popularity contests, but historians believe that he was not as bad as is sometimes thought. Before his career in Australia, he had a distinguished record: he had circumnavigated the globe with Captain Cook, fought under Horatio Nelson at the Battle of Copenhagen, and shown evidence of a superhuman survival instinct when the *Bounty* mutineers abandoned him in the Pacific. Thanks to his courage, his skill as a navigator, and good fortune, he survived a voyage of 5,823km (3,618 miles) in a lifeboat. By coincidence he had also been involved in another serious naval mutiny, in 1797, before being appointed to New South Wales to re-establish discipline. This captain, immortalised by Hollywood, eventually reached the rank of Rear Admiral.

Justice of the Peace. Then he invited some of the others to dinner, much to the horror of the local élite. One of the criminals Macquarie pardoned, Francis Greenway, became the colony's prolific official architect.

Some of the ex-convicts fared so well under Macquarie's progressive policies that he was accused of pampering the criminal class. London ordered tougher punishment, and the total separation of prisoners from the rest of the population. All this led to long-lasting conflict between reformed criminals and their children on one side and a privileged class of immigrants on the other. Nowadays, the shoe is on the other foot: descendants of First Fleet prisoners often express the same kind of pride as Americans of *Mayflower* ancestry.

Many ships were wrecked along New South Wales's rough coasts

The biggest problem for Governor Macquarie and his immediate successors was the colony's position on the edge of the sea. There was not enough land to provide food for the expanding population. The Blue Mountains, which boxed in Sydney Cove, seemed a hopeless barrier. Every attempt to break through the labyrinth of steep valleys failed. Then, in 1813, explorers Blaxland, Wentworth and Lawson had the unconventional idea of crossing the peaks rather than the valleys. It worked.

The Prospector dreams of riches in an 1889 painting

Beyond the Blue Mountains they discovered a land of plenty – endless plains that would support a great new society.

Other adventurers opened new territories. Land was either confiscated or bought from the indigenous tribesmen: for 400 sq km (150 sq miles) of what is now Melbourne, the entrepreneurs gave the Aborigines a wagonload of clothing and blankets plus 30 knives, 12 tomahawks, 10 mirrors, 12 pairs of scissors and 23kg (50lb) of flour. By the middle of the 19th century, thousands of settlers had poured into Australia and all of the present state capitals were on the map.

Age of Gold

In his understandable enthusiasm, rancher Edward Hargraves slightly overstated the case when he declared: 'This is a memorable day in the history of New South Wales. I shall be a baronet.' The year was 1851. The place was near Bathurst, approximately 210km (130 miles) west of Sydney.

Hargraves' audience consisted of one speechless colleague. The occasion was the discovery of gold in Australia.

No sooner had the news of the Bathurst find reached the farthest corner of the land than prospectors from Melbourne struck gold at Ballarat. With two colonies – New South Wales and Victoria – sharing in the boom, adventurers streamed in from both Europe and America. By the year 1860 Australia's population had reached a total of one million. Thirty-three years later the bonanza became a coast-to-coast celebration when gold was discovered in Kalgoorlie in Western Australia.

Life in the gold fields was rugged, aggravated by climate, flies and tax collectors. Whether big winners or, more likely, small losers, all the diggers had to pay the same licence fee. Enforcement and fines were needlessly strict. Justice, the miners felt, was tilted against them. So they burned their licences and demonstrated for voting rights and other reforms. In the subsequent siege of the Eureka Stockade in Ballarat in 1854, troops were ordered to attack the demonstrators. There was heavy loss of life, and the licence fee was abandoned.

Another riot, in 1861, pitted the white prospectors against Chinese miners, who were resented for their foreignness, strong work ethic and frugality. At Lambing Flat, New South Wales, thousands of whites whipped and clubbed a community of Chinese. Police, troops and finally the courts were lenient on the attackers. It was the worst of several race riots. With the tensions of the gold rush, the notion of the 'yellow peril' was embedded in Australia's national consciousness.

Rogues on the Range

Transportation of convicts finally ended in 1868, when London had to admit that the threat of exile in Australia was no deterrent to crime. In Australia itself, crime was always something of a problem; nobody really expected every last sinner to go straight as soon as he arrived. Several wily characters, often escaped convicts, became bushrangers, the local version of highwaymen. They occasionally attracted sympathy from Outback folk because they tended to rob the rich and flout authority. As the crimes grew more ambitious or outrageous, their fame was frozen into legend.

The saga of Ned Kelly (1854–80) reads like Robin Hood gone sour. The Kelly gang preyed on bankers rather than humble ranchers, and Kelly's imaginative operations could be spectacular. But he killed more than his fair share of policemen, almost for the fun of it. Wounded in a shootout, Kelly tried to escape in a suit of homemade armour; this nightmarish contraption deflected most of the bullets, and he was captured wounded but alive. Sentenced to death, he cheekily invited the judge to meet him in the hereafter. Only two weeks after Kelly was hanged, the judge, indeed, died.

An Independent Nation

Having received the blessing of Queen Victoria, the colonies of Australia formed a new nation, the Commonwealth of Australia, on New Year's Day 1901. This federation retained the Queen as head of state, and also bowed to the parliament and Privy Council in London.

Melbourne's shrine to the dead of World War I

Loyalty to the British Empire was tested twice, extravagantly, in the world wars. The Allied defeat at Gallipoli in 1915 was the first and most memorable single disaster for the gallant Australian troops. By the end of World War I, more than 200,000 Australians – two-thirds of the entire expeditionary force – had been killed or wounded.

Combat came closer in World War II, when Japanese planes repeatedly bombed Darwin, enemy submarines penetrated Sydney harbour and sank a ferry (the torpedo had been fired at the American warship USS Chicago), ships were sunk

Anzac Day salutes Australia's role in two world wars

off the Australian coast and a couple of shells hit Sydney's eastern suburbs. American forces under General MacArthur arrived in Australia in 1942 and a US force supported by Australia defeated the Japanese decisively in the Battle of the Coral Sea in May of that year. The statistics: 27,000 Australian servicemen died in action on the European and Asian fronts, and nearly 8,000 more died as prisoners of Japan. Almost one in three Australians taken prisoner by the Japanese died in captivity.

After the war, Britain aligned itself with Europe and downgraded its ties with the old Empire. As Britain's regional power declined, Australia boosted its alliance with the USA. Australian troops (over 40,000 of them) fought alongside Americans in Vietnam, sparking vehement anti-war protests in Sydney and other Australian cities. Australian Prime Minister Harold Holt introduced the draft and promised US President Lyndon B. Johnson that Australia would go 'all the way with LBJ'. Holt disappeared in 1967 while swimming and may have been eaten by a shark.

The tilt towards the USA and Asia also showed up in the trade balance. Prior to World War II, 42 percent of Australia's overseas trade was with Britain. By 1999, Australia's top 10 export markets included Japan, Korea, Taiwan, China, Singapore, Hong Kong and Indonesia. Japan buys almost one fifth of Australia's total merchandise exports. Among non-Asian markets, the most significant for Australian exporters are the USA, New Zealand and Britain.

> **Thanks to its immigrant population, Melbourne is often called the third greatest Greek city, after Athens and Thessaloniki.**

Cultural Changes

Another obvious change in orientation is the racial and national background of Australians. Before World War II, 98 percent of the population was of British or Irish birth or descent. As for immigrants, 81 percent of Australia's overseas-born population came from the main English-speaking countries (Britain, Ireland, New Zealand, South Africa, Canada and the USA.) Since then, the fortress walls of the infamous 'White Australia' immigration policy (enacted in 1901 to maintain racial purity) have been torn down under the slogan 'Populate or Perish.' Australia has seen immigration from many countries including Italy, Greece, the former Yugoslavia, Vietnam, Germany, the Netherlands, the Philippines, Malaysia, Lebanon, Turkey, Hong Kong, China and South Africa.

Australia has accepted more than 470,000 refugees or displaced persons since 1945, creating in the process a culturally diverse nation. About a quarter of Australia's population is overseas-born, a higher proportion than in any other country except Israel and Luxembourg. By June 1999, only 39 percent of the overseas-born population had been born in

English-speaking countries. Despite these statistics, at the beginning of the 21st century Australia's credentials as an open and welcoming society have been severely tested by the government's policy of forcible detention for asylum-seekers.

Australia has had a less than comfortable relationship with its own native peoples. Aborigines (who make up only about one percent of the population) were not permitted to vote in national elections until 1962, and were not included in the census until 1967. Queensland, the last Australian state to grant Aborigines the vote, did so in 1965 – almost a century after African-Americans gained the same right following the US Civil War.

In 1990, a government commission gave native peoples the power to make decisions on social and other matters that affect them. In 1993, the government made further moves towards reconciliation, introducing legislation effectively nullifying the doctrine of *terra nullius* ('uninhabited land'). This colonial policy had deemed Australia to be empty at the time of European settlement and thus, by default, the property of the Crown. The court ruling recognised that Aborigines may hold common law rights or 'native title' to land.

Support continues to grow for a treaty with the

Traditional Aboriginal art depicts the Dreamtime

Aboriginal people to foster national unity. In 2000, in cities throughout Australia, many thousands of citizens marched to demand that the government formally apologise to the Aborigines, to begin a process of reconciliation. In Sydney, 250,000 people marched for the cause. However, the present prime minister, John Howard, has steadfastly refused to apologise to the Aborigines for past wrongs.

Republican Leanings

In the 1990s, prime minister Paul Keating argued that Australia should become a republic, engage strongly with Asia and get rid of Britain's Union Flag from the corner of its own. His successor John Howard is cut from a very different political cloth. He is an ardent monarchist and under his stewardship Australia has looked less towards Asia and more to traditional alliances with Europe and the US.

In 1999, there was a referendum held on whether Australia would become a republic. A prototype republic was put to the vote – and rejected. Opinion polls before and after the referendum show that Australians do, in fact, favour a republic. The problem was that they disliked the model put forward, which proposed that politicians, rather than the people, should elect the president. Australians have always maintained a healthy disrespect for politicians. So Australia entered the new millennium with Britain's monarch on its coinage, a governor general as its head of state, and the Union Jack still adorning its flag.

The Union Jack still occupies a quarter of the Australian flag

Historical Landmarks

50,000 BC   The Aborigines arrive on the Australian continent.

1606   Willem Jansz is the first European to land.

1642   Abel Tasman discovers Tasmania and New Zealand.

1770   Captain James Cook explores the east coast of Australia, which he calls New South Wales.

1788   Britain establishes a penal colony in Sydney Cove.

1808   The 'Rum Rebellion' overthrows Captain William Bligh.

1851   Gold is discovered in New South Wales.

1854   Battle of the Eureka Stockade, Ballarat.

1901   Six colonies federated into the Commonwealth of Australia.

1914–18   330,000 Australians serve in World War I; 60,000 are killed, 165,000 wounded.

1917   Opening of the transcontinental railway.

1927   Federal parliament moves from Melbourne to Canberra.

1928   Royal Flying Doctor Service founded in Queensland.

1939–45   World War II: Australian Air Force active in Britain; navy operates in Mediterranean; 15,000 Australians captured when Singapore falls to Japan; Japanese bomb Darwin.

1956   Olympic Games held in Melbourne. First Australian TV.

1960   Australia grants citizenship to Aborigines.

1962   Aborigines allowed to vote in federal elections.

1965   Australian troops enter the Vietnam War.

1972   'White Australia' immigration policy is abandoned.

1973   Sydney Opera House is finally completed.

1985   Uluru (Ayers Rock), Kata Tjuta (The Olgas) and surrounding desert are returned to Aboriginal owners.

1988   Over 2 million people visit Australia in its Bicentennial year. Queen Elizabeth II opens new Parliament House.

1993   The Aborigines right to own land is recognised.

1999   Referendum rejects prototype republic.

2000   Olympic Games in Sydney.

2001   Australia celebrates the centenary of Federation.

WHERE TO GO

Deciding where to go and what to see in Australia may be the hardest part of the journey. How can you squeeze so much into a limited time? Where to go in such a vast country?

About 29 million passengers a year fly Australia's domestic airline routes, and there are periodic spates of fare discounting. But planning ahead is the best way to ensure low-rate airfares. Alternatives are slower, but often more revealing: try the transcontinental trains and the long-distance buses, some equipped for luxury travel.

Since you probably can't see all of it, you'll have to arrange your tour of Australia to concentrate on touring a manageable slice or two of the continent. Planning your itinerary requires a compromise involving the time and funds you have available, the season, your special interests and your choice of gateway city. Sydney is the major gateway into Australia, but some airlines allow you to arrive in Cairns, for example, and depart from Sydney or Perth.

This section of the guide is arranged according to the geographic reality of Australia's states. Although there is no visible difference between the red deserts of the Northern Territory and those of South Australia, it's convenient to consider them in the context of the political frontiers. Besides, the way that history and chance carved Australia into states comes close to providing a fairly natural division into sightseeing regions.

In each state we start with the capital city gateway and fan out from there. We begin where Australia itself began, at Sydney Cove. After a side trip to the federal capital, Canberra, we continue beyond New South Wales, in an anticlockwise circuit from Queensland to Victoria, ending with a look at the continent's lovely green footnote, Tasmania.

Symbols of Sydney: the Opera House and, beyond, the Harbour Bridge

NEW SOUTH WALES

Sydney can't help but dominate New South Wales, if only because most of the state's population lives in the capital. However, beyond the metropolis, the state – six times the size of England – is as varied as dairyland and desert or vineyards and craggy mountains.

Sydney

Ever since 1788, when the first convoy of convicts arrived to build a new nation, Sydney's harbour has stolen the show. It is so stunning that people alongside are inspired to achievement and *joie de vivre*.

Australia's oldest, liveliest and biggest city (total population 4 million) has good reason for self-congratulation. Its 2000 Olympics were acclaimed as the 'best Games ever' by International Olympic Committee president Juan Antonio

**Sydney's spectacular harbour
seen from the north side**

Samaranch. The Games gave Sydney yet another excuse to party – something that the city does frequently and fervently, as anyone who has witnessed the annual Sydney Gay and Lesbian Mardi Gras parade will affirm. Mardi Gras brings over 500,000 people – by no means all of them gay – onto the streets. It pumps about A$100 million into Sydney's economy.

If the world had a lifestyle capital, Sydney would be a strong contender – something that is richly ironic, considering that the city started out as a British penal colony. Sydney is sun-drenched, brawny, energetic, fun-loving and outdoor-oriented. It ranks highly in world lists of favourite tourist destinations; its residents know this and they revel in it. After hours – and Sydneysiders do live for the after hours – Sydney offers every imaginable cosmopolitan delight. It's a sunny coincidence that beaches famous for surfing and scenery are only a few minutes away.

Most of the world's great cities have a famous landmark that serves as an instantly recognisable symbol. Sydney has two: the perfect arch of Sydney Harbour Bridge and the billowing roofs of the Sydney Opera House. That's what happens when engineers and architects embellish a harbour coveted by artists as well as admirals.

For a quick appreciation of the intricacies of **Port Jackson** (the official name for Sydney Harbour), gaze out from the top of Sydney Tower at Centrepoint, Sydney's tallest building. See the clear blue tentacles of water stretching from the South Pacific into the heart of the city. Schools of sailing boats vaunt the harbour's perfection in the reflection of the skyscrapers, the classic Sydney Harbour Bridge and the exhilarating opera house. It's a pity that Captain Cook never noticed this glorious setting as he sailed right past on his way home from Botany Bay.

Most sightseeing tours – by land or sea – leave from **Circular Quay** (short for Semi-Circular Quay, as it was more accu-

Circular Quay, the terminus for Sydney's many ferries

rately named in olden times). Although cruise ships and water taxis alike dock here, most of the action involves commuter ferries and fast 'Jetcat' catamarans. The quayside's quota of human interest features hasty travellers, leisurely sightseers, street musicians, artists and hawkers. Whether you see Australia's busiest harbour from the deck of a luxury liner, a sightseeing boat, or a humble ferry, don't miss this invigorating angle on the city's skyline.

The Rocks

To start at the beginning, stroll through the charming streets of **The Rocks**, the neighbourhood where Sydney was born. You can take a half-hour guided walking tour (to book, tel: 02-9247 6678) or conduct your own tour. Here modern Australia's founding fathers – convicts who had been charged with anything from shoplifting to major forgery – came ashore in 1788 to build the colony of New South Wales. This historic waterfront district has everything a tourist could want: lovely views at long and short range, moody old buildings, cheerful plazas and plenty of distractions in the way of shopping, eating and drinking.

But it nearly was not so. Until comparatively recently, The Rocks was one of Sydney's most squalid and dangerous quarters, a Dickensian warren of warehouses, grog shops and brothels, where the rum was laced with tobacco juice and the larrikin 'razor gangs' preyed on the unwary. An outbreak of bubonic plague in 1900 was a low-light in The Rocks' sordid history.

The whole area was due to be levelled for redevelopment in the 1970s, but there was fierce resistance from residents and academics, and the project was thwarted when the construction unions, led by activist Jack Mundey, refused to start work. This was the beginning of the Green movement to preserve whatever was atmospheric about Old Sydney.

Pick up local leaflets and maps at **The Rocks Visitors' Centre** (open: daily 9am–5pm), 106 George Street. You can book tours there as well. This building also has an interesting history – it was built in 1907 as the Coroner's Court.

Cadman's Cottage, next door, is Sydney's oldest (1816) surviving house – a simple stone cottage occupied for many years by the government's official boatsman. Not far away, the **Museum of Contemporary Art** (open: daily except Tues, 11am–6pm) gives new life to an Art Deco building formerly used by the Maritime Services Board. Few other art museums enjoy such a view. Displays change regularly and the café on the terrace is excellent.

Walking north from Cadman's Cottage past solid old bond stores, now converted to offices and shops such as **Campbell's Storehouse** (eating, souvenirs, arts and crafts), you'll arrive at the **Argyle Cut**, a massive

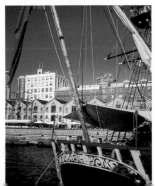

The Rocks, where the first convicts disembarked in 1788

excavation hacked with pickaxes through sandstone cliffs by convict labour-gangs. At the top of Argyle Cut, Cumberland Street provides access to Sydney Harbour Bridge via **Cumberland Steps**. In Cumberland Street not far away, the **Australian Hotel**, a friendly pub in the older Aussie tradition, stocks beers from every state in the country. The Australian is one of only two pubs in Sydney to serve unfiltered beers created by master brewer Geoff Scharer. They are acclaimed by expert tasters as possibly the best beers in Australia.

A little further on, in Argyle Place, you will find a neat row of terraced houses straight out of Georgian England. Two other grand old pubs in this area deserve mention. The quaint **Hero of Waterloo** at 81 Lower Fort Street was built in 1843 on top of a maze of subterranean cellars through which drunken patrons were conveyed to be sold as crew to unscrupulous sea captains. That practice has died out but the cellars remain.

The **Lord Nelson**, a square sandstone block of a building at the corner of Kent and Argyle Street, was built c1840 and has maintained a British naval atmosphere ever since. It brews its own beers, some of them pretty potent.

For history without the refreshments, visit the Garrison Church, officially named the **Holy Trinity Anglican Church**, which dates from the early 1840s. As the unofficial name indicates, it was the church for members of the garrison regiment, the men in charge of the convict colony. It's now a fashionable place to get married.

At the start of George Street, close to the Irish-influenced Mercantile Hotel, **The Rocks Market** (Sat–Sun 10am–5pm) takes place every weekend under a 150-m (492-ft) long canopy. Musical groups and street entertainers perform, while stall-holders sell crafts, leatherwear, souvenirs, toys and gifts. Not far away, Customs Officers Stairs lead down to some charming harbourside restaurants housed in old bond stores, fronting **Campbells Cove**.

Overhanging The Rocks, **Observatory Hill** is a perfect place from which to gaze at the sky or at Sydney Harbour. This is the highest point of the city, visible for miles around. Since the middle of the 19th century, at 1pm precisely every day, a ball is dropped from the top of a mast for the benefit of sea captains who want to to check their chronometers. The 125-year-old **Sydney Observatory** (open: daily 10am–5pm) is now a museum of all things astronomical, and opens every evening (times vary according to season) for talks, films and star-gazing.

Another favourite lookout point is **Dawes Point Park**, a verdant hill with a scattering of ancient cannons, from where you can watch the comings and goings of the ferries, hydrofoils and sailing boats in the harbour.

Here, you're in the shadow of **Sydney Harbour Bridge**, 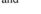 with its drive-through stone pylons (purely ornamental) and

Ancient warehouses have been converted into chic restaurants

The majestic Harbour Bridge from the terrace of the Opera House

colossal steel arch. The bridge stars on television each New Year's Eve, when it serves as a platform for a spectacular fireworks display. To bid farewell to 1999 and welcome in 2000, hundreds of fireworks were fired from the arch in a spectacular computer-controlled sequence. Other fireworks positioned on the road-span created a Niagara-like cascade into Sydney Harbour, while the bridge lit up with the word 'Eternity' – the word scrawled in chalk on Sydney sidewalks for nearly 40 years by a reformed petty criminal who died in 1967.

Linking the city and the north, the bridge's single arch is 503m (1,650ft) across, and wide enough to carry eight lanes of cars and two railway tracks, as well as lanes for pedestrians and cyclists. When it was built, during the Great Depression, Sydneysiders called the bridge the Iron Lung, because it kept a lot of people 'breathing' – in economic terms. It takes ten years to repaint the bridge, at the end of which it's time to start again. To ease traffic congestion a tunnel has also been built under the harbour.

An unusual vantage point for viewing the bridge, the harbour and the skyline is from the top of one of the bridge's massive pylons. The **lookout** (open: daily 10am–5pm) is in the southeast tower, and the stairway can be reached via Cumberland Street, The Rocks.

A company called BridgeClimb (tel: 02-9252 0077) conducts guided walks for small groups over the bridge's massive arches. Not across the walkway below, but over the arches above. For decades, groups of daredevils have been doing this illicitly. Since the legal climb began in 1998 the waiting list has grown quite long and it pays to book your climb as far in advance as you can. You can even do the climb at night, though excursions are understandably postponed during electrical storms. It's not a cheap thrill: tickets cost around A$175 (concessions available).

City Centre

Sydney Tower at Centrepoint (open: Sun–Fri 9am–10.30pm, Sat 9am–11.30pm) is the city's highest vantage point, at 305m (1,001ft) above the street. Some locals regard it as an eyesore, but there's no denying the quality of the views from the top. It takes only 40 seconds to reach the observation decks, where amateur photographers get that glazed look as they peer through the tinted windows to unlimited horizons. On a flawless day you can see all the way north to Terrigal and south to Wollongong,

In 1932, at the opening ceremony of the Harbour Bridge, the leader of a fanatical right-wing group, Francis Edward de Groot, rode up on a horse and sliced through the ribbon with a sword before the left-wing prime minister, Jack Lang, could cut it.

far out to sea to the east, or as far west as the Blue Mountains. Otherwise, look out and down at the seething shopping streets all around the tower.

One of the streets below is the city's main square, **Martin Place**, flanked by the imposing Renaissance-style Victorian **General Post Office** (GPO) building. This has been imaginatively converted into a stylish modern complex including a 418-room, five-star Westin hotel. The ornate GPO façade has been retained. During World War II, the clock tower was dismantled for fear that Japanese bombers might zero in on the landmark. The clock was restored 20 years later.

The controversial Sydney Tower has great views from the top

From the same era as the GPO, but even grander, the **Queen Victoria Building** (open: daily 9am–6pm, Thur 9am–9pm) occupies an entire block on George Street (Sydney's main street and the oldest street in Australia) opposite Sydney Town Hall. The Byzantine-style 'QVB' began as a municipal market and commercial centre, including a hotel and a concert hall, topped by statuary and 21 domes.

Built in 1898 to commemorate Queen Victoria's Golden Jubilee, it was condemned to demolition in the 1960s by small-minded officials, to make way for a parking garage. Fortunately, the authorities ran short of money, the demolition was put on hold and the building was faithfully restored in the 1980s to create a magnificent all-weather shopping centre housing nearly 200 chic boutiques, cafés and restaurants, in a cool and unhurried atmosphere of period charm. Pierre Cardin called it 'the most beautiful shopping centre in the world'.

Shop in style in the byzantine Queen Victoria Building

Next door, Sydney's **Town Hall** (open: daily 9am–5pm) enlivens a site that used to be a cemetery. The Victorian building, home of the city council, is also used for concerts and exhibitions. **St Andrew's Cathedral** next door, Anglican and newly renovated, is the oldest cathedral in Australia.

Chinatown

After dark, young Sydneysiders flock to the section of George Street heading south from the Town Hall, lined with video entertainment arcades, fast-food joints and a cinema complex. Sydney's fledgling Latin Quarter begins nearby on the corner of George Street and Liverpool Street – there's a choice of tapas bars here.

In the adjacent Chinatown district, gourmets can enjoy the delights of Peking, Cantonese and Szechuan cuisine. The substantial local Chinese community is joined by Sydneysiders and tourists enjoying the Chinese cafés, restaurants and shops selling exotic spices and knick-knacks. The district's centrepiece is **Dixon Street**, a pedestrian zone framed by ceremonial gates.

If you're here at the weekend, check out **Paddy's Market** (open: Thur 10am–6pm, Fri–Sun 9am–4pm), a cavernous brick building beneath a new skyscraper. Paddy's is full of stalls selling almost anything: souvenirs, seashells, sunglasses, fruit, vegetables and semi-antiques. On level three of the same complex you'll find **Kam Fook Shark's Fin Seafood Restaurant**, a Chinese eatery so vast that its waiters use mobile phones to converse with the kitchen staff.

Nearby **Darling Harbour** is well stocked with shops, restaurants and attractions, and a **monorail** system links it to more central areas. On the city side of Darling Harbour is **Cockle Bay**, a complex of bars and restaurants. This has proved much more popular than the shopping and dining complex overlooking the harbour on the western side, mainly because Cockle Bay is easier to reach on foot from downtown Sydney.

Not far away, **Sydney Aquarium** (open: daily 9am–10pm) is one of the largest in the world. In its Open Ocean Oceanarium, large sharks weigh up to 300kg (660lb) and measure over 9m (30ft) long. The Great Barrier Reef Complex houses over 6,000 creatures, and a visit there is the closest thing to diving on the reef without getting wet.

Other nearby attractions include the **Sydney Maritime Museum** (open: daily 9.30am–7pm), designed by Sydney architect Phillip Cox to resemble billowing sails, and the 12,550-seat **Sydney Entertainment Centre**, which is used for sports events and concerts.

Parks and Gardens

Although Sydney's lush **Hyde Park** is only a fraction the size of its namesake in London, it still provides the same sort of green relief. Like most big-city parks, however, it should be avoided after sunset. The most formal feature of the semi-formal gardens, the **Anzac War Memorial**, commemorates

The monorail links Darling Harbour to downtown Sydney

the World War I fighters in monumental art deco style, with later acknowledgments to the World War II contingent.

Sightseers interested in old churches should mark a few targets on the edge of Hyde Park. To the north, the early colonial **St James's Church** in Queens Square was the work of the convict architect Francis Greenway. Just across College Street on the east, **St Mary's Cathedral** stands on the prominent site of the colony's first Catholic church. The sandstone spires at the southern end are new: although they were included in the original plan in 1865, they were not added until just before the 2000 Olympics and are hence somewhat lighter in colour than the original spires.

You can view the spires while immersed in a swimming pool next door at **Cook and Phillip Park** (open: Mon–Fri 6am–10pm, Sat–Sun and Bank Hols 7am–8pm). This aquatic, fitness and recreation centre opened in 1999. You can't readily see the complex from the street, yet when you're inside its huge windows give views and let in lots of light. There are three pools – one with a wave machine. There's a café inside, or, if you want to eat alfresco, Bodhi's vegan restaurant does good business just outside.

The ornate **Great Synagogue** faces the park across Elizabeth Street. Jews have lived in Sydney since the arrival of the first shipment of prisoners.

The **Australian Museum** (open: daily 9.30am–5pm) on College Street specialises in natural history and anthropology. On the second floor in a glass tank, you may even find a couple of live specimens of the world's largest cockroach. The giant burrowing cockroach *(Macropanesthia rhinoceros)*, native to Australia, lives in woodland and feeds on dead eucalyptus leaves, growing up to 10cm (4in) long and weighing up to almost 50g (1¾oz) – or about the weight of an AA-size battery. Don't miss the 'Bone Ranger' skeleton display or the large Museum Shop downstairs.

The restored **Hyde Park Barracks**, (open: daily 10am–5pm) designed by Greenway, located between Hyde Park and the Botanic Gardens, is now a museum of social history. On the top floor of the barracks, one large room is a reconstruction of the dormitory life of the prisoners. The **Mint**, next door, processed gold-rush bullion in the mid-19th century.

Another large park adjacent to Hyde Park is called the **Domain**. For a century or so, it has been home to Sydney's equivalent of Speaker's Corner, where anyone can climb aboard a soapbox and make a speech, in London's Hyde Park; Sunday is the day of the orators and hecklers. The **Art Gallery of New South Wales** (open: daily 10am–5pm) consists of a formal exterior decorated with much bronze statuary and a modern extension, added in 1988, which infuses light into the building and provides sweeping views of east Sydney, part of the harbour, and the suburb of Woolloomooloo.

An afternoon at the Art Gallery will give you a crash course in more than a century of traditional and modern Australian art. The **Yiribana Gallery** there is devoted to Aboriginal art and Torres Islander art, and has performances of Aboriginal music and dance (noon Tues–Sat).

Sydney's **Royal Botanic Gardens** (open: daily 7am–sunset; free guided walks daily at 10.30am) began as a different sort of garden: here the early colonists tried – with very limited success – to grow vegetables. Only a few steps from the busy skyscraper world of downtown Sydney, you can relax in the shade of Moreton Bay fig trees, palms or mighty mahoganies, or enter a glass pyramid full of orchids and other tropical beauties. The gardens curve up around Farm Cove to a peninsula with the quaint name of **Mrs Macquarie's Point**. The lady thus immortalised, the wife of the go-ahead governor, used to admire the view from here; now it's better than ever.

Centennial Park, most easily reached from the eastern end of Oxford Street in the inner-city suburb of **Paddington**, has provided greenery and fresh air to city folk since 1888, when it was dedicated on the centenary of Australia's foundation to 'the enjoyment of the people of New South Wales forever'.

The Domain lies between Farm Cove and Woolloomooloo Bay

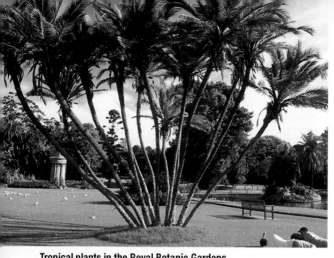

Tropical plants in the Royal Botanic Gardens

Centennial Park's 220 hectares (544 acres) of trees, lawns, duck ponds, rose gardens and bridle-paths are visited by about three million people a year, who cycle, roller-blade, walk their dogs, feed birds, play team sports, throw frisbees, fly kites, picnic and barbecue seafood or sausages.

Centennial Park, and **Lachlan Swamp** within it, support large numbers of birds. Species include distinctive long-beaked ibises, which are native to Australia despite looking as exotic as birds etched on the walls of ancient Egyptian tombs. Flocks of loud-squawking, sulphur-crested cockatoos make their presence known, bats twitter in the park's venerable Moreton Bay fig trees, and possums live in the date palms. The palms themselves are under threat from a mysterious virus and are being progressively replaced with more resistant species.

If you fancy a ride on the bridle path, horse rental can be arranged from Moore Park Stables (tel: 02-9360 8747).

Bicycles and pedal-carts can be hired from Centennial Park Cycles (tel: 02-9398 5027). **Centennial Park Kiosk**, a lovely setting for a meal and a glass of wine, was renovated and expanded in 1998. Beside it stands a charming, if curious, modern stone fountain.

Centennial Park Amphitheatre provides an outdoor venue for events and productions. In the summer months, a popular Moonlight Cinema programme is held there. Films start at about 8.45pm, and tickets are available at the gate from 7.30pm. For screening details, tel: 1900 933 899.

Sydney Opera House

There's a real sense of occasion and style about the familiar structure of the **Sydney Opera House**, both inside and out. ◄ This unique building, covered in a million tiles, has achieved the seemingly impossible by improving a virtually perfect harbour. Yet its controversial architect left the country in a huff at an early stage of construction.

Until the arrival of the opera house, the promontory was wasted on a fancy, turreted depot for tramcars, and in the 1950s the government of New South Wales decided to build a performing arts centre on the site. A Danish architect, Jørn Utzon, won an international competition to design the building, and his novel plan included problems of spherical geometry so tricky that he actually chopped up a wooden sphere to prove it could be done.

The shell of the complex was almost complete when Utzon walked out; the interior, which was in dispute, became the work of a committee. Despite this, from the tip of its highest roof (67m/220ft above sea level) to the Drama Theatre's orchestra pit (more than a fathom below sea level), this place has grace, taste and class.

The name 'Sydney Opera House' is as renowned worldwide as it is inaccurate. The actual opera theatre is only one of the centre's five, and it is not the biggest. Note that if you're 'fashionably late' for the opera, there is no admission until the first intermission, probably the end of the first act. It's worth taking a guided tour of the whole building. Tours depart about every 30 minutes between 9am and 4pm every day except Christmas Day and Good Friday.

Kings Cross

East of the Domain is the district of **Woolloomooloo** (the name has something to do with kangaroos in an Aboriginal language). A spelling teaser for Australian school children, Woolloomooloo was threatened by wholesale demolition in the 1970s, but was saved by resident protests and union 'green bans'.

East of Woolloomooloo, bright lights and shady characters exist side by side in Kings Cross, a couple of railway

The striking 'sails' of the Opera House

stops from Circular Quay. 'The Cross', as it's often called, is Sydney's version of Pigalle, in Paris, or London's Soho – neon-filled, a bit tacky but rather fun, crawling with hedonists of all persuasions. Action continues 24 hours a day, with a

> The initial budget for the Opera House was A$7 million. By the time it was opened by Queen Elizabeth II in 1973, it had cost A$102 million. A state lottery raised most of the cash.

diverting cavalcade of humanity – the brightly coloured, the bizarre, the grotesque, the stoned, the happy and the drunk. On weekends, tourists flock to the Cross to glimpse a bit of weirdness. Sometimes though, the weirdest characters they spot are other tourists.

The Cross's 'main drag' (major street) is **Darlinghurst Road**, bohemian verging on sleazy and dotted with a jumble of bars, strip joints, fast-food outlets, tattoo parlours and X-rated book and video shops. The **Bourbon and Beefsteak Bar** is a fun place for a few drinks, though rather touristy these days. It was highly popular with American servicemen on R&R leave in the 1960s during the Vietnam War.

Kings Cross is famous (or infamous) for its 'spruikers' (pronounced *sprookers*) – fast-talking salesmen who hang around the doors of strip clubs and try to lure passers-by inside. Predictably, their main targets are single men or men in groups. They tend to leave mixed-sex couples or mixed-sex groups alone.

This area also offers reputable hotels and shops, a fountain commemorating the World War II desert battle of El Alamein, and good ethnic restaurants.

A five-minute walk from Kings Cross Station brings you to **Elizabeth Bay House** (open: Tues–Sun 10am–4.30pm), a stately home built in 1835 and a reminder that the Kings Cross precinct was once highly respectable.

If you have time for one more inner suburb, make it **Paddington**, to the south-east of Kings Cross. Its trademark is the intricate wrought-ironwork, known as Sydney Lace, on the balconies of 19th-century terraced houses. This feature, and the rather bohemian atmosphere, reminds some travellers of New Orleans. After decades of dilapidation, the district came up in the world rapidly as a fashionable, rather artsy place to live. It has developed into one of Sydney's most sought-after suburbs, with house prices to match. 'Paddo', as the locals like to call it, offers plenty of ethnic restaurants, antiques shops, art galleries, fashionable bookshops and trendy boutiques. One of Sydney's best public markets, **Paddington Bazaar**, is held 10am–4pm every Saturday on the grounds of Paddington Public School in Oxford Street. It offers every type of art and craft and is enlivened by a variety of street entertainers.

Typical wrought-iron balconies in the Paddington district

Paddington's main street, **Oxford Street**, is a centre for Sydney's large gay community, with the Albury the street's longest-established gay pub. The Street is home to two of Sydney's best bookshops, Ariel and Berkelouw, and three of its more imaginative cinemas, the Chauvel, the Verona and the Academy Twin. **Victoria Barracks** is Oxford Street's renowned example of the mid-19th-century military architecture, built by convicts to house a regiment of British soldiers and their families.

Around Sydney Harbour

Take a harbour cruise to appreciate hidden beaches, islets, mansions old and new, even a couple of unsung bridges. Various companies run half-day and full-day excursions. Or you can rent a boat of your own in which to weave around the rest of the nautical traffic.

Fort Denison, situated on a small island, is graphically nicknamed 'Pinchgut.' Before the construction of a proper prison, the colony's more troublesome convicts were banished to the rock to subsist on a bread-and-water diet. In the middle of the 19th century the island was fortified to guard Sydney from the far-fetched threat of a Russian military strike. Ironically, the only attack came in World War II when an American warship, conducting target practice, hit old Pinchgut by mistake.

Taronga Zoo (open: daily 9am–7pm), a 12-minute ferry ride from Circular Quay, boasts a superb setting. Over the heads of the giraffes you can see across the harbour to the skyscrapers of Sydney. The zoo's Nocturnal House features indigenous night-time creatures illuminated in artificial moonlight, unaware of onlookers. The Rainforest Aviary houses hundreds of tropical birds. If you arrange your visit around feeding times, which are posted at the gate, you can watch the keepers distribute food while they deliver talks about their charges.

Vaucluse House (open: Tues–Sun 10am–4.30pm), a stately home with its own beach, adds its mock-Gothic turrets and battlements to the skyline. The splendid, 15-room mansion, begun in 1803, is run by the state's Historic Houses Trust. It can also be reached by bus or taxi.

Further afield, both north and south of Sydney, are miles of inviting beaches. **Manly** got its name when the first governor of the colony thought that the Aborigines sunning themselves on the beach looked manly. This pleasant north-shore resort has back-to-back beaches that are linked by the Corso – a lively promenade full of restaurants and tables for picnickers.

Bondi (pronounced *bond-eye*), is a favourite with surfers and an Australian icon. The varied characters on the sand range from ancient sunworshippers to bathing beauties, and include a remarkable number of New Zealanders. Note that if a warning bell clangs on the beach, it signifies a shark alert; the alarm may be false but you shouldn't assume this.

Bondi's main promenade, Campbell Parade, is lined with dozens of restaurants and one pub, the **Bondi Hotel**, open until 4am six days a week and until midnight on Sundays.

Olympic Sydney

The Sydney 2000 Olympic and Paralympic Games are history but the euphoria lingers as Sydneysiders fondly remember their city's moment in the limelight. Athletes coined the phrase 'the Games of Smiles'. Observers from around the world remarked how Australians cheered spontaneously for all teams and competitors, not just their own side. After US sprint star Marion Jones won her three gold medals, Marion's mother (who visited Sydney with her family for the Games), was moved to write to the *Sydney Morning Herald* to thank Aussie fans who, even when Marion beat Australian contenders, 'applauded Marion at the end, respected her, afforded her the dignity and the courtesy which I have never seen anywhere else. Thank you Australia, and thanks for loving my daughter Marion.'

Now the Games are over, Sydney's magnificent, purpose-built Olympic Park is somewhat under-employed. Critics call it a white elephant, and say it will be at least a decade before

The golden sands of Bondi, Australia's best-known beach

the facility becomes self-sufficient and can cover its costs. Other cities have encountered similar post-Games challenges.

The Park is still fun to visit and you can swim at the excellent **Aquatic Centre**. Allow a full day if you want to visit each venue at the site; otherwise, half a day is probably enough. The best way to get there is to catch a Parramatta Rivercat ferry from Circular Quay. These depart hourly and give a 50-minute scenic river trip before you alight at Homebush and catch an Olympic Explorer bus.

The graceful, parabola-shaped centrepiece of Olympic Park, **Stadium Australia**, (open: daily 9.30am–5.30pm, hourly guided tours 9.30am–3.30pm), was Sydney's premier Olympic venue, hosting the Opening and Closing Ceremonies, the track and field programme and the closing stages of the Marathon. The Stadium is the largest ever built for Olympic Games.

A giant new park called **Millennium Parklands** has been created from 450 hectares (1,112 acres) of land around the

Olympic facilities and the new Sydney Showground that adjoins it. Bigger than New York's Central Park and twice the size of Sydney's pre-existing Centennial Park, Millennium Parklands was one of very few large parks to open within a major world city in the 20th century.

Before the park and the Olympic facilities could be built, a massive clean-up of the site was required. It had previously served as a saltworks, brickworks, abattoir, naval armaments depot and landfill dump. Native foliage has been replanted and a more natural creek system recreated, with meandering pools to encourage wildlife to return. Studies show that birds and fish are coming back, including a regular visitor to Homebush Bay, the Golden Plover, which flies a 22,000-km (13,670-mile) round trip to Australia from Alaska each year.

The **Olympic Village**, a short walk from Stadium Australia, was built to house the Olympic athletes. It's now one

Stadium Australia was purpose-built for the 2000 Olympics

of Sydney's newest environs, billed as 'the world's most environmentally friendly village'. In fact it's the world's largest solar-powered suburb, with the capacity to generate more than a million kilowatt-hours of power annually.

The **Sydney International Aquatic Centre** (SIAC; open: Mon–Fri 5am–7.45pm, extended to 8.45pm Apr–Oct) welcomes athletes, community groups, overseas visitors and families for watersports, recreational swimming, carnivals and fun. Although not built specifically for the Games, it was certainly in the right place. Four pools include one for leisure, complete with palm trees and mosaics, encompassing five spas, a river ride, spray jets, spurting 'volcanoes', a water slide and bubble beach.

Sydney Showground, next to the main Olympic site, attracted 1.2 million people to the first Royal Easter Show held there in 1998. The Showground's environmentally passive, ingeniously designed halls and pavilions minimise the need for air-conditioning and heating.

Excursions from Sydney

Within day-trip distance of Sydney – by car, train, or sightseeing bus – a choice of scene-changers shows the big variety of attractions offered by New South Wales. Any of the most popular outings will deepen your understanding of Australia and its assets.

The Blue Mountains

A 90-minute trip to the west of Sydney by road brings you to the **Blue Mountains**, a scenically dramatic region of forested ravines and pristine bushland that recently gained a World Heritage listing. As well as its scenic and environmental value, the Blue Mountains offer a wealth of adventure activities, art and craft galleries, and romantic escapes in grand country lodges or cosy bed and breakfasts.

The name 'Blue Mountains' derives from the mountains' distinctive blue haze, produced by eucalyptus oil evaporating from millions of gum trees. Well-marked walking trails criss-cross Blue Mountains National Park, passing streams and waterfalls, descending into cool, impressive gorges, and snaking around sheer cliffs. This breathtaking environment is easily reached from Sydney, either by road or on a two-hour rail journey. Trains run there several times daily from Central Station.

➤ The region's best-known rock formation is The **Three Sisters**, a trio of pinnacles best viewed from **Katoomba**, the largest of 26 mountain towns. **Katoomba Scenic Rail**, the world's steepest railway, descends from the cliff-top at Katoomba down into the Jamison Valley. You can walk down a series of steps by the Three Sisters, stroll along a cool and refreshing trail and catch the Katoomba Scenic Rail to the top. Above, the Skyway carries passengers along a cableway 206m (675ft) above the valley floor.

Katoomba's **Maxvision** giant screen is a relatively recent Blue Mountains innovation. It shows *The Edge – The Movie*, a gripping presentation of Blue Mountains environment, history and ecology. You'll learn about the Wollemi Pine, the world's oldest species of tree. Unique to the Blue Mountains, this ancient genus of pine was discovered in 1994 by the New South Wales National Parks and Wildlife Service. The tree's closest relations became extinct during the Jurassic and Cretaceous periods between 65 and 200 million years ago. As one Sydney-based botanist exclaimed at the time, 'This is like finding a living dinosaur in your backyard.

For more than a century, spelunkers, hikers and ordinary tourists have admired the **Jenolan Caves**, at the end of a long, steep drive down the mountains from Katoomba. Guided tours through the spooky but often awesome limestone caverns last about an hour and a half. The atmosphere is cool in summer, warm in winter, and always damp. For more information, tel: (02) 6359 3311.

Old Sydney Town

North of Sydney, beyond the sparkling waters of the Hawkesbury River, history buffs can visit a reconstruction of the original penal colony, Old Sydney Town. Here budding actors in period costumes duel, march, fire musket and cannon, flog convicts, and generally keep themselves busy amusing and informing visitors to the site. It's a hugely entertaining and educational day out. The best idea is to arrive at about 10am and follow the action around. If you get bored you can always go next door and spend the rest of the day marvelling at the **Australian Reptile Park** (open: daily 9am–5pm).

On the way to Old Sydney Town, the Pacific Highway cuts through **Ku-ring-gai Chase National Park**. This compact area of unspoiled forests, cliffs and heathland is home base for numerous species of animals and birds. But you have to find them for yourself; it's not a zoo. The Aborigines who lived in this area long before the foundation of New South Wales left hundreds of rock

The Blue Mountains' most famous peaks, the Three Sisters

This viewpoint offers a fabulous close-up of the Three Sisters

carvings – pictures of animals and supernatural beings. The information centre has maps pinpointing the locations of the most interesting carvings.

Hunter Valley

Australia is one of the world's major wine-producing countries. The Hunter Valley, a two-hour drive from Sydney, is the premier wine-growing area of New South Wales. The Hunter's 50 wineries harvest grapes in February and March and welcome visitors throughout the year. The gateway to the Pokolbin region, where the majority of the Lower Hunter Valley wineries are located, is **Cessnock**, 195km (121 miles) north of Sydney, where the tourist information centre supplies touring maps and brochures.

Most of the Hunter wineries are open for cellar-door tastings. Some of the major establishments include Tyrell's Wines, Lindemans Winery, Wyndham Estate, the Hunter

Estate, the Rothbury Estate and the McWilliams Mount Pleasant Winery.

Newcastle, the commercial centre of The Hunter, is located approximately 170km (106 miles) to the north of Sydney. It's a coalmining and shipbuilding centre, and also offers well-developed recreational possibilities on the Pacific, the **Hunter River** and the saltwater **Lake Macquarie**. The lake, which is popular with weekend sailors and fishermen from far afield, is said to be the largest seaboard lake in Australia.

Further north, **Port Stephens** offers safe swimming beaches, a range of water activities and good fishing. Its bay is home to dozens of bottlenose dolphins, which can be viewed up close on a cruise.

In the far north of New South Wales, **Byron Bay** provides wonderful beaches and great surf. It's a haven for alternative lifestylers – a few of them very rich.

Lord Howe Island

In the South Pacific, 483km (299 miles) east of Port Macquarie, Lord Howe Island, the state's off-shore possession, is said to be the world's most southerly coral isle. This makes for splendid snorkelling and scuba diving. Lord Howe Island has been on the UNESCO World Heritage list since 1982. If you prefer to stay dry you can go out in a glass-bottom boat. There are also numerous walking trails, many birds and some unique vegetation.

Forests, beaches, mountains and all, Lord Howe Island only amounts to a speck in the ocean – around 1,300 hectares (3,220 acres) – with a population of approximately 300 and a couple of cars. Bicycles and motorbikes are ideal for getting around this part of the country, as the roads are very quiet. You can fly out from Sydney to this sleepy lagoon in a couple of hours.

The Snowy Mountains

If you've come to Australia in search of snow, you need go no further than the southeastern corner of New South Wales. Skiing in the Snowy Mountains is usually restricted to the months of July, August and September. But even in the antipodean summer a few drifts of snow remain to frame the wild flowers of the Australian Alps. At the top of this world is **Mt Kosciuszko**, at 2,228m (7,308ft) high, named after an 18th-century Polish patriot by a 19th-century Polish explorer. This is the birthplace of three important rivers, the Murray, the Murrumbidgee and the Snowy.

Kosciuszko National Park is made up of approximately 6,300 sq km (2,432 sq miles) of the kind of wilderness you won't see anywhere else: buttercups and eucalyptus and snow, all together in the same breathtaking panorama. The only thing missing is a pine tree, or any of the other familiar

Cape Byron is the most easterly point of Australia

conifers of the Northern Hemisphere. Cars must be equipped with snow chains from 1 June to 10 October. However, even during the summer months the weather can change for the worse at very short notice, so be sure always to carry a warm, waterproof jacket. The best-known ski resorts in this area are **Thredbo** and **Perisher Valley**.

New South Wales Outback

Although New South Wales is the most populous and productive state (in both manufacturing and farming), it extends to the infinities of Australian Outback – bushland and cattle stations seem thousands of kilometres from commuterland.

Dubbo is the sort of place where the Old Gaol, meticulously restored, is a prime tourist attraction, gallows and all. Just out of town, the **Western Plains Zoo** is advertised as Australia's only open-range zoo, a cageless convention of koalas, dingoes and emus, plus more exotic (to Australians) animals like giraffes, zebras and monkeys.

Lightning Ridge, in the Back of Beyond near the Queensland border, enjoys one of the most evocative of Outback names. Fortune hunters know it well as the home – reputedly the only home – of the precious black opal. Tourists are treated to demonstrations of fossicking, and there are opportunities to shop for opals.

Bourke is a small town whose name signifies the loneliness of the Outback, where dusty tracks are the only link between distant hamlets. 'Back of Bourke' is an Australian expression for really far-out Outback. Bourke looks a lot bigger on the map than on the ground.

Broken Hill (population more than 23,300) is about as far west as you can go in New South Wales, almost on the border with South Australia. It's so far west of Sydney, there's a half-hour time difference, even though both are in the same state. The town is legendary for its mineral wealth –

it has produced millions of tons of silver, lead and zinc. Tourists can visit the mines, either underground or on the top. The neatly laid-out town, with its streets named after various minerals – Iodide, Kaolin, Talc – has become an artistic centre, with works by Outback painters on show in numerous galleries. Pro Hart, one of Australia's best-known and most prolific painters, is a long-time Broken Hill resident.

CANBERRA

Australia lived up to its reputation when it came to picking the site for a national capital. Out of conflict emerged a green and pleasant compromise, far from the pressures of the big cities. Where sheep had grazed, the young Commonwealth raised its flag.

When the new nation was proclaimed at the turn of the 20th century, the perennial power struggle between Sydney and Melbourne reached an awkward deadlock. Each of the cities offset its rival's claim to be the national capital. So they carved out a site in the rolling bush 320km (200 miles) southwest of Sydney, and it soon began to sprout clean white official buildings, followed by millions of trees and shrubs. As compromises go, it was a winner.

To design a model capital from scratch, Australia held an international competition. The prize was awarded in 1912 to the American architect Walter Burley Griffin. He had grand designs, but it took longer than anyone imagined to transfer his plan from the drawing board to reality, owing not only to the distractions of two world wars and the Depression, but also to a great deal of wrangling. Burley Griffin, a Chicagoan of the Frank Lloyd Wright school, put great emphasis on coherent connections between the settings and the buildings, and between landscape and cityscape.

At the heart of the Australian Capital Territory, Canberra has a population of about 300,000. Although the city is an educational and research centre, it's essentially a company town: the local industry is government. The ministries are here, and the parliament with its politicians, lobbyists and hangers-on, and the foreign embassies. The Royal Military College Duntroon, Australia's first military college, founded in 1911, is based in Canberra, as is the Australian Institute of Sport. In spite of this considerable enterprise, Australia's only sizeable inland city is uncrowded and relaxed.

City Sights

There are several good ways to see Canberra – but not on foot. As on any map of Australia, the distances are greater than you think. If you do want to walk, many of the main attractions are found near Lake Burley Griffin – but you'll still need three or four hours. It's a good idea to sign up for a bus tour; they come in half-day and all-day versions. Or take Murray's Explorer bus, which runs a 25-km (15-mile) route stopping at all the main sights. You buy an all-day ticket, then hop on and off at will. Alternatively, you can drive yourself around the town, following itineraries that are

Anzac Parade and, across the lake, Parliament House

mapped out in a free sightseeing pamphlet available from the Canberra Visitors Centre (Northbourne Avenue, Dickson; tel: 02 6205 0044). In the middle of town, Travellers Maps and Guides is located in the Jolimont Centre, Northbourne Avenue; tel: (02) 6249 6006.

An effective starting place for a do-it-yourself tour is **Regatta Point**, which overlooks the lake that Burley Griffin cleverly created in the middle of town. Man-made **Lake Burley Griffin**, 35km (22 miles) around, is generously named after the town planner who realised the value of water for recreation as well as scenic beauty. You can currently enjoy fishing, sailing and windsurfing here, and plans for sightseeing boats are in the works. Whooshing up from the lake, a giant **water jet** honours the explorer Captain Cook for several hours each day (10am–noon and 2pm–4pm, plus 7pm–9pm during summer). The **Carillon**, another monument rising from Lake Burley Griffin (actually from a small island), was a gift from the British government. Apart from concert recitals, it tells the time every 15 minutes, taking its tune from London's Big Ben.

North of the Lake

To get the big picture, have a look at the view from the **Telstra Tower** (open: daily 9am–10pm) atop **Black Mountain**. Millions of sightseers have paid to ascend the 195-m (640-ft) tower for the 360-degree perspective. A viewing platform circles the structure towards the top, and the designers couldn't resist adding a café and a revolving restaurant. If you want to eat there, you'll have to book ahead – tel: (02) 6248 6162.

On the eastern slopes of Black Mountain, the **National Botanic Gardens** (open: daily 9am–5pm) are entirely devoted to Australian flora – they have the most comprehensive collection anywhere. In spite of Canberra's mostly mild,

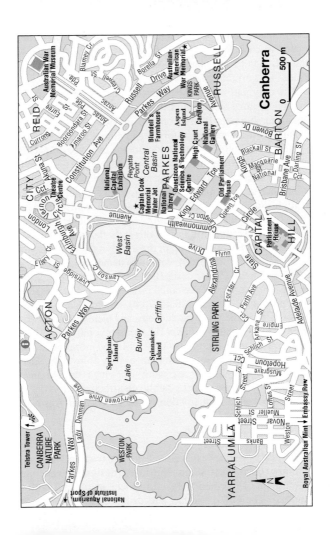

dry climate, numerous rainforest specimens flourish under intensive care. Walter Burley Griffin was so fascinated by the native trees and plants of Australia that he included this place in his original plan.

The only part of the capital designed with pedestrians in mind is the area around the **Civic Centre**. The original business and shopping district opened in 1927 – by Canberra standards that's ancient history – and comes complete with symmetrical white colonnaded buildings in a mock-Spanish style. Nearby are modern shopping malls, the **Canberra Theatre Centre**, and an historic merry-go-round.

A more conventionally styled dome covers the vast **Australian War Memorial**, which is a sandstone shrine climaxing a ceremonial avenue called **Anzac Parade**. There are war memorials all over Australia, but this is the definitive one. It's hard to avoid being swept up in the mood of the place as you walk past walls inscribed with the names of more than 100,000 Australian war dead. But beyond the heroic statues and mosaic murals, the memorial is the most-visited **museum** in Australia (open: daily 10am–7pm), with displays of uniforms through the years, battle maps, and plenty of hardware, from rifles to a real World War II Lancaster bomber.

Closer to the lake is one final military monument: the **Australian-American Memorial**, a slim aluminum shaft supporting a stylised eagle with its wings upheld in a victory V. It was paid for by public contributions in order to acknowledge US participation in the defence of Australia during World War II.

South of the Lake

The mostly windowless walls of the **Australian National Gallery** (open: daily 10am–5pm) were designed to enclose 'a museum of international significance,' as official policy decreed. The enterprise has succeeded on several levels,

The vast Australian War Memorial at the head of Anzac Parade

showing off artists as varied as Monet and Matisse, Pollack and de Kooning, and an honour roll of Australian masters. Another indication of the range of interests are the displays of art from Pacific island peoples, black Africa and pre-Columbian America.

One of the high points is the collection of Australian Aboriginal art: intricate human and animal forms on bark, evolving into the modern version in polymer paint on chipboard, dots and whorls and crosshatching looking at first glance like arbitrary abstractions. The gallery also has a glistening sculpture garden overlooking Lake Burley Griffin.

The **High Court of Australia** (open: daily 9.45am–4.30pm), linked to the National Gallery by a footbridge, is a bold, boxy building with an immense expanse of glass on its façade and a waterfall. This last stop for legal appeals bears no resemblance to the Victorian halls of justice elsewhere in the country. But the building is no less impressive for its unconventional looks. Its huge public hall is sometimes used for exhibitions and concerts.

One of Canberra's best known landmarks is 'Questacon,' or the **National Science and Technology Centre** (open: daily 10am–5pm), a hands-on science museum. Architecturally, it's an interesting study in curves. The low-slung copper-plated dome rests on graceful arches standing in a circular moat. Some say it looks like a flying saucer at rest.

Also on the lakefront, the **National Library** (open: daily 9am–5pm) houses more than 2 million books. This institution serves scholars and other libraries, and mounts exhibitions of rare books. Its reading room houses an extensive selection of overseas newspapers and magazine publications. There are guided tours, a bookshop, and a pleasant café, the Brindabella Bistro.

Canberra's new Parliament House was opened in 1988

Canberra's neo classical **Old Parliament House** became the seat of government in 1927 and fulfilled that role until it was replaced in 1988. It is now the home of the **National Portrait Gallery** (open: daily 9am–5pm). Outside it is the **Aboriginal Tent Embassy**, erected to protest that Aboriginal land rights have not been achieved.

A new, permanent parliament building to replace the old one was dedicated by

Queen Elizabeth II in the bicentennial year, 1988. **New Parliament House** can be visited daily 9am–5pm, and there are free guided tours. The interior represents the best in Australian art and design. The Great Hall is dominated by a tapestry 20m (66ft) high. The combination of an unusual design as well as exploding building costs made the new complex, on the site originally selected by Burley Griffin, a surefire *cause célèbre* during its construction. Taxpayers noted the lavish offices, bars, swimming pool and sauna.

Meanwhile, they're minting it in the southwestern district called Deakin, and you can take a look for yourself. The **Royal Australian Mint** (open: Mon–Fri 9am–4pm, Sat–Sun 10am–4pm) has a visitors' gallery overlooking the production line where the country's coins are punched out. The factory also 'moonlights' to produce the coins of several other countries. The Mint's own museum contains coins and medals of special value.

Other Canberra attractions include the **National Film and Sound Archive** and the **Australian Institute of Sport**, which includes an interactive sports exhibition called Sportex. There are guided tours of the Institute every day starting at 10am, 11.30am, 1pm and 2.30pm.

What's in a Name?

The name of Australia's new capital city, which is said to be derived from 'meeting place' in an Aboriginal tongue, was officially chosen in 1913 from among a huge outpouring of suggestions. Some of the more serious citizens wanted to have a name as uplifting as Utopia or Shakespeare. Others devised classical constructions, for example Auralia and Austropolis. The most unusual proposal was a coinage designed to soothe every state capital: Sydmeladperbrisho. After that mouthful, the name Canberra came as a relief.

Out of Town

Animal lovers don't have far to go to meet kangaroos, echidnas, wombats and whatnot. The **National Aquarium and Australian Wildlife Sanctuary** (open: daily 9am–5.30pm) is only a few miles southeast of the city centre, in Red Hill. You can walk through acrylic tunnels while sharks cruise past. The bird population includes parrots, kookaburras (the large, noisy kingfishers), cockatoos and emus.

The **Tidbinbilla Nature Reserve** (open: daily 9am–6pm), 40km (25 miles) southwest of Canberra, is a much bigger affair – thousands of acres of bushland where the native flora and fauna, including kangaroos, wallabies and koalas, flourish. Next to this unspoilt wilderness, the **Tidbinbilla Deep Space Tracking Station** (open: daily 9am–5pm), one of only three deep-space tracking stations in the world, operated in conjunction with the US space agency NASA. Tidbinbilla has several exhibitions on space exploration.

See (and hear) kookaburras at the Australian Wildlife Sanctuary

ACT's Outpost

Thanks to a bit of historical gerrymandering, landlocked Canberra has a toehold on the South Pacific. **Jervis Bay**, a peninsula located on the New South Wales coast, was annexed to the Australian Capital Territory early in the 20th century on the off-chance that the future Canberra might need a seaport. It didn't, however. The coastal enclave today includes an uncommon combination of facilities: inviting dunes and beaches rub shoulders with the Royal Australian Naval College, a missile range and a National Park. Jervis, named after an English admiral, is correctly pronounced 'Jarvis', although locals are starting to rhyme it with nervous. The sand on Jervis Bay beaches is dazzling white. Dolphin cruises operate from the town of **Huskisson** – you almost always get to see dolphins, and sometimes migratory whales as well. Not far away, a delightful glade called **Greenpatch** offers some remarkably tame wildlife and multicoloured birds.

One of the bay's unusual sights is the wreck of the **Cape St George Lighthouse**. The placement of this 19th-century beacon was unfortunate. It was built in the wrong place, virtually invisible to northbound ships. Even worse, the construction itself was considered to be a hazard to navigation. To remedy the situation, the navy took aim and reduced it to an historic ruin.

QUEENSLAND

Queensland provides just about everything that makes Australia so desirable, plus some spectacular exclusives of its own. Sun-soaked Queensland gives you the choice of flashy tourist resorts, Outback mining towns or a modern metropolis; rainforest, desert or apple orchard. But the most amazing attraction of all is Queensland's offshore wonderland – the longest coral reef in the world, the Great Barrier Reef.

Queensland is one of those typical Australian success stories. It was founded in 1824 as a colony for incorrigible convicts, the 'worst kind of felons', for whom not even the rigours of New South Wales were a sufficient deterrent. In an effort to quarantine criminality, free settlers were banned from an 80-km (50-mile) radius.

But adventurers, missionaries and hopeful immigrants couldn't be held back for long. Queensland's pastureland attracted many eager squatters, and in 1867 the state joined the great Australian gold rush with a find of its own. Prosperity for all seemed to be just around the corner.

Mining still contributes generously to Queensland's economy. Above ground, the land is kind to cattle and sheep, and warm-hearted crops like sugar, cotton, pineapples and bananas. But tourism is poised to become the biggest money-spinner, for Queensland is Australia's vacation state, welcoming tourists to wild tropical adventurelands in the far north, and the sophistication of the Gold Coast in the south. The busiest gateways to all of this are the state capital, **Brisbane**, and the port of Cairns, which has become one of Australia's most popular tourist destinations.

Brisbane

As befits a subtropical city with palm trees and back-garden swimming pools, Brisbane's pace is so relaxed you'd hardly imagine its population was more than a million. The skyscrapers, some quite audacious, have gone a long way towards overcoming the 'country-town' image, but enough of the old, elegant, low-slung buildings remain as a reminder of former days; some are wonderful filigreed Victorian monuments, some done up in bright, defiant colours.

In 1859, when Brisbane's population was all of 7,000, it became the capital of the newly proclaimed state of Queensland. The state treasury contained only 7½ pence, and within a couple of days even that was stolen. Old habits of the former penal colony seemed to die hard.

The capital's location, at a bend in the Brisbane River, has made possible some memorable floods over the years, but it

Australia's third city Brisbane enjoys a subtropical climate

sets an attractive stage for Australia's third-largest city. Spanned by a network of bridges (the first dated 1930), the river continues through the suburbs to the beaches and islands of Moreton Bay. Some of Australia's most celebrated types of seafood come from here, notably the gargantuan local mud crabs and the Moreton Bay bug. Despite its name, this creature, related to the lobster, is a gourmet's joy.

Up the hill, on Wickham Terrace, stands an unusual historic building, the **Old Windmill**, also known as the Old Observatory, built by convicts in 1829. Design problems foiled the windmill idea; to grind the colony's grain, the energy of the wind had to be replaced by a convict-powered treadmill. Later, the tower found less strenuous uses as a fire lookout station and a transmitter for early television experiments.

King George Square, next to City Hall, and the nearby **Anzac Square** are typical of the green open spaces that make the centre of town breathable. Pedestrians-only is the rule in Brisbane's central **Queen Street Mall**, flanked by big stores and interspersed with shady refuges and outdoor cafés. This is a place for people-watching. Here, on a fine day, visitors from cooler climes should take a seat to enjoy the warm sun and watch the passers-by. The local men go about unselfconsciously in sport shirts and shorts – except for businessmen, wilting in suits and ties.

Where central Brisbane fits into the bend in the river, the **Botanic Gardens** (open: daily 8am–5.30pm) turn the peninsula green with countless species of Australian and 'exotic' trees, plants and flowers. **Parliament House** (open: Mon–Fri 9am–5pm when parliament is not sitting, Sun 10am–2pm), a political hothouse built in the 19th century in Renaissance style, overlooks the gardens and is the headquarters of the state's legislative assembly.

Across the Victoria Bridge from the centre of town, the **Queensland Cultural Centre** puts most of Brisbane's cultural eggs in one lavish, modern basket. The south-bank complex includes the **Queensland Art Gallery** (open: daily 10am–5pm), the **Queensland Museum** (open: daily 9.30am–5pm) and the **Queensland Performing Arts Centre**, consisting of the 2,000-seat Lyric Theatre, a 1,800-seat concert hall and smaller performance spaces. The riverside gardens, plazas, restaurants and cafés round off the scene. There are free guided tours of the Performing Arts Centre (Mon–Fri at noon).

If you're looking for a classic Brisbane pub, check out the **Breakfast Creek**

Brisbane's Old Windmill

Hotel on the north side of a bend in the Brisbane River. It was built in 1889. If you seek bars and restaurants, **Fortitude Valley** is a lively precinct. Brunswick Street, the valley's main thoroughfare, is lined with nightclubs, street cafés and arty, sometimes scruffy, little shops. There's an Irish pub and a compact **Chinatown**. At weekends a market

King George Square and City Hall

operates. Nightlife there can be fun, but it's wise to take a taxi heading home after dark.

The site of the 1988 World Expo, **South Bank Parklands**, has put many of the former Expo pavilions to innovative use. Its attractions include the **Gondwana Rainforest Sanctuary**, as well as a diverse array of restaurants that take full advantage of the city's weather. This is the place to head for on a sunny day, for an outdoor meal. Brisbane, once a culinary desert, now enjoys a reputation for chefs who make good use of their state's natural resources: giant mud crabs, ripe avocados, macadamia nuts, mangoes, barramundi, coral trout and oysters, as well as exotic tropical delights. You may wish to bring your swimsuit: South Bank even has a large swimming lagoon at **Kodak Beach**, complete with sand.

To escape the heat and rush of the city, try **Mt Coottha Forest Park**, on the western edge of Brisbane. The name is derived from an Aboriginal word meaning 'mountain of dark honey'. The spacious park features a giant modern dome enclosing 200 species of tropical plants. Here, too, you'll find Australia's largest **Planetarium** (programmes Wed–Fri at 3.30 and 7.30pm, Sat–Sun 1.30 and 3.30pm).

It's only about 11km (7 miles) to **Lone Pine Sanctuary** (open: daily 8.30am–5pm), which is home to one of the country's best-known collections of native animals. By boat the trip is a few miles longer. The stars of the show are the koalas, mostly sleeping like babies, clinging to their eucalyptus branches. The sanctuary has kangaroos galore. This is also a golden opportunity to get a close-up look at Tasmanian devils, which are red-eared, mousy-looking marsupials the size of a small pig and, unlike the koalas, difficult to fall in love with.

Recent developments for visitors include a self-guided tour along the **Albert Street Literary Trail** (a series of 32 bronze plaques bearing quotes about Brisbane) and **St Helena by Night**. The latter attraction involves participants boarding a vessel (ominously called the *Cat o' Nine Tails)* at dusk, donning prisoners' garb and setting out from Manly on Moreton Bay for St Helena Island, Queensland's former prison.

The islands of Moreton Bay, some unpopulated, make this a vast fishing and sailing paradise. **Moreton Island** features **Mt Tempest**, at 285m (935ft) the world's highest stabilised coastal dune. On **North Stradbroke Island**, the island's Aboriginal community has developed a 90-minute tour called the **Goompi Trail**. An Aboriginal guide explains the island's flora and fauna, with Dreamtime stories, bush tucker (food) and medicine.

The koala is Queensland's official mascot. Its only occupation is eating eucalyptus leaves, the odour of which impregnate its whole body, providing both anti-septic protection and a deterrent to predators.

The Gold Coast

South of Brisbane, a day-trip distance if you're rushed, the **Gold Coast** is a Down Under impression of Miami Beach. Although it may be overexploited, it's so dynamic and there are such a lot of opportunities for things to do that you can hardly fault it. And the beach – anything from 30 to 50km (19–31 miles) of it, depending on who's doing the measuring – is a winner in any league. More than 20 Gold Coast surfing beaches patrolled by surf lifesavers form the backdrop for activities ranging from swimming, sailing and boating to surfboarding and windsurfing.

The trip down the Pacific Highway south from Brisbane (78km or 49 miles and about an hour's drive) is a study in Australian escapism. In the midst of forest and brushland grows a seemingly incxhaustible supply of amusement parks,

The koala was once hunted for its fur but is now a protected species

luring transient fun-seekers with attractions for all the family: these diverting parks – there are seven major ones – have names like Dreamworld, Sea World, and Wet 'n' Wild and operate from 10am to 5pm every day. **Warner Bros Movie World**, one of the biggest, offers a Hollywood-style experience – the only Hollywood theme park in the southern hemisphere – including stunt shows, special effects and large-format amusement rides.

The **Dreamworld** park operates an attraction claimed to be 'the fastest, tallest ride in the world', the Tower of Terror. Visitors thrill to action-packed rides with names like Wipeout and Thunderbolt, watch adventure films on a six-storey-high screen or (if they want something quieter) cuddle a koala. Other Gold Coast theme attractions include **Sea World** (open: daily 10am–5.30pm), noted for its dolphin displays, and **Wet 'n' Wild** (open: from 10am daily, closing times vary throughout the year), which contains a giant wave pool, a 45-degree toboggan water drop and a seven-storey speed slide. And if the heat gets to you at the beach, incredibly at **Frozen World** you can spend a maximum of 20 minutes enjoying unique ice carvings, ice slides and snowball fights.

Nature-lovers can also enjoy **Currumbin Sanctuary** (open: daily 8am–5pm), where masses of squawking rainbow lorikeets are fed each morning and evening.

Currumbin is down towards the southern extremity of the Gold Coast, which ends at **Point Danger** (so named by Captain Cook when he passed by in 1770). Beyond lies New South Wales.

The essence of the Gold Coast is **Surfer's Paradise**, as lively as any seaside resort in the world and much addicted to high-rise living. When you're not sunbathing, swimming or surfing, you can go bungee jumping next to Sea World or just window-shop, eat out, socialise or wander through the malls, one of which, **Raptis Plaza**, is adorned by a full-scale replica of Michelangelo's *David*. The pace is hectic, and the revelry goes on as late as you can last. To unwind, take a leisurely boat cruise along the Southport Broadwater or canals of Surfer's Paradise.

A new Surfer's Paradise landmark, not far from Sea World, is **Palazzo Versace**, the world's first Versace Hotel, billed as 'six star' and filled with Versace trappings.

Surfer's Paradise is approached through a thicket of petrol stations, fast-food outlets and motels – a reconstruction of the outskirts of many an American city, and in similar taste. The conglomeration is skyscrapered in a peculiar way: tall, slim apartment blocks interspersed with bungalows. The high-rise skyline of Surfer's must now rank with Ipanema, Miami and Cannes for architectural overkill. The tanned, relaxed 'beautiful people' you see on the beach today were probably pale, tense office-workers a couple of days ago; the irresistible sun does wonders.

The lush green backdrop to the Gold Coast is known as the Hinterland. It encompasses subtropical rainforests, waterfalls and bushwalking tracks, mountain villages and guest houses, craft galleries and farm-stay accommodation.

The Sunshine Coast

For the beachy perfection of the Gold Coast with less commercialism (although they're working on it), try the resorts of the **Sunshine Coast**, north of Brisbane. Some of Australia's best surfing is hiding here.

Feed the rainbow lorikeets at Currumbin Sanctuary

The resort closest to Brisbane, **Caloundra**, has a beach for every tide. The northernmost town on the Sunshine Coast, **Noosa**, used to be a sleepy little settlement, the weekend haunt of local farmers and fishermen. That was in the 1960s, before the surfers, then the trendsetters from Sydney and Melbourne arrived. But it's still laid back. **Noosa National Park**, a sanctuary of rainforest and underpopulated beaches, occupies the dramatic headland that protects Laguna Bay from the sometimes squally South Pacific breezes. Fraser Island *(see page 89)* is easily reached from here.

This whole stretch has some of Queensland's most gorgeous coastline. Beaches such as **Maroochydore** and **Coolum** are gems. Inland, the territory is laden with vast plantations of sugar cane, bananas, pineapples and passion fruit. The area is also a centre of production of the prized macadamia nut.

Near **Nambour**, the principal town inland from the Sunshine Coast, you can hardly miss a terribly Australian sort of tourist attraction: the monstrously magnified symbol. A startling example is an immense fibreglass replica of a pineapple, as tall as a house – the come-on for a whole tourist complex. A competitor in this field of the ridiculous is the 9-m (30-ft) high Big Cow, so colossal that you are

Skyscrapers and watersports on the Gold Coast

invited to climb inside. The valley of the giants also includes a cartoon Aussie boozer, the Big Ettamogah Pub. The new **Sunshine Highway** from Brisbane to Noosa bypasses these gargantuan attractions, except the pub; the others are accessible from an off-highway **Nambour Tourist Drive**.

The Great Barrier Reef

Australia's biggest and most wonderful sight, the **Great Barrier Reef**, lies just below the ocean waves. Many millions of minuscule cells multiply relentlessly in fantastic shapes, growing into an infinite variety of forms – and colours from lettuce green to flaming crimson – to create the world's largest living phenomenon. The reef is home to 400 different types of coral. It stretches as far as you can see and beyond: more than 2,900km (1,430 miles) of submerged tropical gardens. In among them, the sea is sprinkled with hundreds of paradise islands.

The giant reef was proclaimed a marine park by the Australian Government in 1975, and placed on the World Heritage list in 1981, becoming the biggest World Heritage area in existence. It is now managed by the Great Barrier Reef Marine Park Authority.

Seen more intimately through a diver's mask, the reef is the spectacle of a lifetime, like being inside a boundless tropical fishbowl among the most lurid specimens ever conceived. The fanciful shapes of the coral, gently waving in the tide, might almost lull you to sleep. But not for long. A blazing blue-and-red fish darts into sight, pursuing a cloud of a thousand minnows. A sea urchin stalks past on its needles; a giant clam opens its hairy mouth as if sighing with nostalgia for its youth, a century ago.

In 1770 Captain Cook was exploring the Australian coast and stumbled upon the Great Barrier Reef: the *Endeavour* was gored by an unsuspected outcrop of coral. Patching the holes as best they could, the crew managed to sail across the barrier, and the vessel limped onto the beach at what is now Cooktown, where some major repairs had to be improvised.

There are many ways of appreciating the coral and its fishy visitors. You can stay dry in a glass-bottom boat, or join a brief cruise aboard a semi-submarine. Or descend into an underwater observatory at the Townsville **Great Barrier Reef Wonderland**, which includes the world's largest coral reef aquarium.

Equipped with just a mask and snorkel you can get close to the underwater world, but the only way to blend totally with the environment is in a weightless state, diving as long and as deep as you please with scuba gear. If you're not a qualified diver you can take a crash course at many of the resorts. Organised excursions for advanced divers are also available.

In some places the coral stands exposed, but visitors are asked not to walk over it, as that severely damages the living organisms.

The Reef Islands

The reef – actually a formation of thousands of neighbouring clumps of reefs – runs close to shore in the north of Queensland but slants ever further out to sea as it extends southwards. Hundreds of islands are scattered across the protected waters between the coral barrier and the mainland. More than a dozen have been developed into resorts, ranging from spartan to sybaritic. But only two resort islands – Heron and Green – are on the reef itself. From all the others you

Not all of the reef's islands are made of coral. In fact, most of the popular resort islands are the tips of offshore mountains. True coral cays are smaller and more fragile.

A snorkel and flippers are all you need to explore a coral wonderland

have to travel, by sea or air, from 5 to 70km (3 to 43 miles) to reach the main attraction. Here are some details about the character and facilities of the resorts of the Great Barrier Reef, heading from south to north:

Fraser Island is actually south of the Great Barrier Reef but it is close enough to it, and interesting enough, to rate inclusion in this list. About 120km (75 miles) long, Fraser is considered to be the largest sand island in the world. But there's more than sand: lakes, marsh, pine forest and rainforest. This is an island for fishing and beachcombing, not swimming or coral dives. Excursions to the island are available from Noosa *(see page 85)*.

Lady Elliot Island is a coral isle, part of the reef, but situated south of the Tropic of Capricorn. Activities centre on diving, swimming and windsurfing. The gateway airport is in Bundaberg, a sugar-producing town 375km (230 miles) up the coast from Brisbane.

Heron Island is heaven for divers. It's a small coral island right on the Great Barrier Reef. Amazing coral and hundreds of species of fish are waiting to be sighted just outside your door. Alternatively, nature-lovers can concentrate on the giant green turtles, which waddle ashore between mid-October and March to bury their eggs in the sand. Heron Island is also the goal of thousands of migrating noddy terns and shearwaters. A resort on the island accommodates up to 250 people. There are no day trips and no camping.

Great Keppel Island is one of the larger resort islands in area and in tourist population. The great white beaches are simply gorgeous. The Great Barrier Reef is fully 70km (44 miles) away, but Great Keppel is surrounded by good local coral, and there's an underwater observatory. Its beaches are among the best in the resort islands. Great Keppel is also one of the cheapest islands to reach from the mainland – a return

Lake McKenzie is just one of Fraser Island's freshwater lakes

ferry trip from Rosslyn Bay costs about A$30. For other angles on the sea's secrets in the area, rent a sailboard, catamaran, motorboat and/or snorkelling gear from the Beach Shed on Putney Beach. You can also go water-skiing or parasailing.

Brampton Island, an informal resort, is easily reached by air or sea from Mackay. With forested mountains and abundant wildlife, it's worth exploring the mountainous interior of the island. You can also discover neighbouring Carlisle Island, uninhabited and connected to Brampton by a reef that is wadeable when the tide's out. If the many sandy beaches don't suffice, there's a saltwater swimming pool.

Lindeman Island, the most southerly of the islands in the Whitsunday archipelago, was named by Captain Cook after the feast of Pentecost, which is approximately the time of year when he passed through. Lindeman Island was almost overrun by feral goats, but they have been eradicated. If you want an all-inclusive vacation you can stay at the Club Med Resort there. There's a campsite as well. You can travel there by boat or fly in with Island Air Taxis from Whitsunday Airport on the mainland.

With its jet airstrip, 14-storey apartment tower, seven restaurants, 10 bars, a 200-boat marina and the largest freshwater pool in the Pacific, **Hamilton Island** is the slickest international resort in the Coral Sea. It's all carefully thought out, from the busy yacht marina and shops to the landscaping around the Polynesian-style cottages. Divers can rush out to the reef by catamaran or by helicopter. The island's rainbow lorikeets not only eat out of your hand but sit on your arm while doing it. There are tame kangaroos, too.

Long Island is 11km (7 miles) long – narrow and hilly. Close to the mainland and far from the reef, it has three resorts: Club Crocodile, Long Island Palm Beach Hideaway and Whitsunday Wilderness Lodge. There's also a campsite. Most of the island is national park rainforest.

Hamilton is the largest of the Whitsunday Islands

South Molle Island also consists mainly of national park, plus a resort. South Molle is virtually joined to North Molle Island 2km (1¼ mile) away, and to the closer Mid Molle Island. The beaches are good (there are some quiet ones at the south), and you'll find nice paths for walks through the hilly bush. The Great Barrier Reef is 60km (37 miles) away but coral reefs still exist nearby.

Daydream Island is the tiniest of all the Barrier Reef resort islands, snoozing just offshore from busy Shute Harbour. Since beaches are not the island's strongest selling point, Daydream Island International Resort has built swimming pools. The resort accommodates 300 guests. A day trip to the island from Shute Harbour costs approximately A$25.

Hayman Island, the most northerly of the Whitsunday group, boasts the chic, international-class Hayman Island Resort, a lavish, five-star hotel. Hayman has a marina for drop-in yachts, and a choice of restaurants, bars and shops. The long, sandy beach suggests all sorts of watersports, dutifully organised for guests by the resort's activities staff. Some tiny, uninhabited isles are so close you can walk out to them at low tide.

Magnetic Island is virtually a suburb of Townsville, the biggest city in northern Queensland. Many of the island's 2,500 or so permanent residents commute to work on the mainland by ferry. Being so easy to reach, it's a busy daytrip destination – by sea or helicopter – but Magnetic Island also has plenty of accommodation of all classes. Most of the island is a national park, busy with birds and animals (including koalas in the gum-trees), and the choice of beaches is enticing. Magnetic Island, 'Maggie' to the locals, was given its name by the omnipresent Captain Cook, whose compass malfunctioned here.

Famous visitors to **Orpheus Island** have included Zane Grey and Vivien Leigh half a century ago. Over 100 species of fish and 340 of the 350 known species of Reef coral adorn underwater gardens in the island's several sheltered bays, with the channel at the southern point of Orpheus believed to host the Reef's largest range of soft corals. **Orpheus Island Resort**, the longest-established resort on the Great Barrier Reef, is one of the few remaining privately owned Australian island resorts. Nestling in a sheltered bay on the western (mainland) side of the island, the resort accommodates a maximum of 74 guests in 31 private rooms. Day-trippers and children under 15 are banned.

Hinchinbrook Island basks in a superlative of its own: 'The world's largest island national park'. A continental rather than coral island, but only 5km (3 miles) from the reef, Hinchinbrook has a couple of campsites (park rangers issue permits on the mainland) and a small resort with 65 rooms. Inland from the smooth sand beaches, you will find mountains well worth climbing, as well as rainforest, waterfalls and bushland, where you'll come across wallabies.

Bedarra Island, in the Family Islands group, accessible via neighbouring Dunk

All shades of blue at luxury Hayman Island Resort

Island, has a very small, exclusive, and expensive resort on its west coast. It costs over A$1,000 a day to stay there, all inclusive. The nearest mainland town is Tully, noted for its annual rainfall average, the highest in the country. Statistically, Tully is twice as wet as Darwin.

Dunk Island is mostly a national park, but one of the best developed resorts fits inoffensively into a corner of the island originally occupied by a World War II radar station. Dunk's genuine tropical rainforest offers a taste of the eternal: vines struggling to grab the sunlight at the expense of the trees they strangle on the way up. All is silence except for a waterfall, the trickle of raindrops off glistening leaves, the fluttering wings of a brightly plumed bird.

In the interior you can visit the carefully tended grave of Edmund Banfield, the island's first white resident. A journalist from Townsville, Banfield went to the island in 1898 to die quietly, having been given only weeks to live. He survived for 25 more years, writing books with titles including *The Confessions of a Beachcomber* and *My Tropic Isle*.

Fitzroy Island came into the resort business later than most. It's only 6km (4 miles) offshore and easily reached on day excursions from Cairns. Lodging here is quite limited, but a dining room and regular evening entertainment keep the overnight population well amused. Fitzroy is totally surrounded by coral reef, and has rainforest in the interior; the beaches meet anyone's standards, however high. Nudey Beach is one of the best.

Green Island, one of the two resorts actually on the reef, is, like Fitzroy, popular with day-trippers from Cairns, but when the crowds depart, the vacationers occupying the five-star Green Island Reef Resort have the tiny island, and its throngs of seabirds, to themselves. The resort takes 92 guests. Green Island's Underwater Observatory, which claims to be the first of its kind in the world, lets you view the coral garden from the dry, three fathoms below water level. In this situation, the fish come to look through the glass at human beings in the tank. Another attraction, a short walk inland, is Marineland Melanesia, with crocodiles, stingrays, giant turtles and Melanesian artefacts.

Lizard Island, situated about 30km (19 miles) off the tropical northern coast of Queensland, has all the trappings of a fictional escape island, with rainforest, mangrove swamps and a couple of dozen delectable beaches. The island is almost on the edge of one of Australia's most productive

Many islands of the Reef have good mooring for leisure sailors

game-fishing zones, in which the half-ton black marlin are found. It's favoured by millionaires and celebrities, who stay at the exclusive and pricey Lizard Island Resort. The only other alternative is a very basic campsite.

The Tropical Coast

The coast of mainland Queensland that is parallel to the Barrier Reef terminates in the north with Cape York Peninsula, one of Australia's wildest and least populated areas. If you're heading there, it's best to go with an experienced operator – roads are often little more than dirt tracks. Here are a few highlights further south, from south to north, heading along the Capricorn Coast relentlessly towards the Equator.

Rockhampton sits only a few kilometres north of the Tropic of Capricorn – 23°27' south of the Equator, and the line that officially divides the tropics from the subtropics. From here on northwards, you need no excuse to order an icy beer to assuage your tropical thirst. Rockhampton, known as the beef capital of Australia, has some genuinely interesting Victorian architecture, and is worth a walking tour. To the north, the Berserker Range offers spectacular limestone caves.

Mackay is the next substantial town, and even by Australian standards it's a long haul – about 340km (210 miles) – over Highway 1, a road not particularly noted for its scenery. Surrounded by dense fields of cane, Mackay processes one-third of the nation's sugar crop. At the harbour stands the world's biggest bulk sugar terminal. From July to December you can see cane crushing in progress at the **Farleigh Sugar Mill**, about 12km (7 miles) northwest

---

Perils of the Deep – and the Shallows

Take care when you explore the Reef: some species of coral can cause very painful burns. The crown-of-thorns starfish may also be lying in camouflaged ambush for you: its thousands of long, sharp spines are seriously poisonous.

But between December and April, perhaps the greatest threat of all comes from the box jellyfish ('stingers'). In summer these small, transparent, almost invisible creatures swarm along the north Queensland coast in their thousands – and their sting can be fatal. All the popular beaches have stinger net enclosures, along with vinegar for medication in case a tentacle gets through, but you should always heed the warning signs.

of the town on the Bruce Highway. The largest national park in Queensland, **Eungella National Park**, lies inland from Mackay, in rugged mountain country. This is one of the few places in Australia where you can see platypuses in the wild. The best time is morning and late afternoon and there's a platypus viewing platform near the bridge in Eungella township.

The tropical rainforest of Mossman Gorge, near Cairns

Proserpine, another sugar town, is situated inland from **Airlie Beach** and **Shute Harbour**, resorts from which there are boat trips to the Whitsunday Islands.

Another 265km (165 miles) closer to the Equator, and you reach the metropolis of Queensland's far north, **Townsville** (population about 128,000), named after Robert Towns, a Sydneysider. Townsville is the headquarters of the mining and cattle industries of Queensland's interior and one of the gateways for islands of the Reef. The historic centre of town, along the river, contains some photogenic old buildings with filigreed iron balconies or stately columns and arches. Townsville's top attraction is the **Great Barrier Reef Wonderland** (open: daily 9.30am–5pm), with a superb simulation of the reef and a fantastic, colossal aquarium.

The landscape changes from dry to lush as you head north to **Cairns**, Townsville's regional rival. Cairns (population about 114,000) is likely soon to replace Townsville as Australia's largest tropical city. A port laid out in grid style with huge blocks and extra-wide streets, Cairns has benefited economically from Australia's tourist boom and grown dramatically, but in the process has lost much of its former sleepy, tropical outpost atmosphere. It's an ideal base for regional exploration, within reach of the Great Barrier Reef, the World Heritage-listed Daintree rainforest, the temperate Atherton Tableland, the Outback and even Cape York.

Some 600 tour options are available in Cairns every day and the city has become Australia's foremost centre for adventure tourism. No fewer than three hot-air balloon companies operate locally, plus skydiving and numerous whitewater rafting operations. Diversions in Cairns itself include the **Pier Marketplace** (a shopping and leisure complex), the **Reef Hotel Casino** (four separate gaming areas and a five-star hotel), and **Undersea World Oceanarium**, providing visitors with an introduction to the Great Barrier Reef. The region's largest shopping complex, **Cairns Central**, is on the corner of McLeod and Spence Streets. It contains 180 speciality shops on three levels, a food court and an entertainment centre with six cinemas.

Cairns action begins early in the morning, when speedy catamarans leave for Green Island and Fitzroy Island and smaller boats set sail with scuba divers or fishermen aboard. Big-game fishing for black marlin is big business in Cairns.

Some travel agencies open their doors at 7.30am and keep going until after dark. They sell a large collection of excursions – to Green Island, inland to Kuranda and the Atherton Tableland, and up the coast as far as Port Douglas.

The lovely little tourist town of **Kuranda**, 'the village in the rainforest', with its craft shops, galleries and restaurants, is located a short distance northwest of Cairns. Kuranda is linked to Cairns by two fascinating transport systems: the wonderfully quaint and picturesque **Kuranda Scenic Railway**, and the **Skyrail Rainforest Cableway**, which transports visitors to Kuranda in six-person aerial gondolas over dense, tangled World Heritage-listed rainforest. You can buy tickets for a round trip – train one way and Skyrail the other. Skyrail riders can enter the forest on boardwalks at two stations on the way up and view trees from there. A rainforest information and research centre is located at Barron Falls Station. The Skyrail experience is even better when it's misty or raining and the gondolas fill with a woody aroma as mists rise from below. Sweeping views of sugarcane plantations, the Coral Sea, beaches and offshore islands give way to eucalyptus forest and later to the massive fig trees, kauri pines, and twisted vines of the 120-million-year-old rainforest.

The **Tjapukai Aboriginal Cultural Park** at the base of Skyrail is home to the world-renowned Tjapukai Aboriginal Dance Theatre. Performances are primal and electrifying (for bookings, tel: 07-4042 9900). The **Australian Woolshed** has opened in the same complex, offering visitors an experience of life on an Australian farm.

Spectacularly beautiful coastal scenery is the reward along the highway north from Cairns to **Port Douglas**. When the tide is out, Port Douglas's Four Mile Beach is a wide, hard-packed, almost flat sweep of

The Kuranda Scenic Railway more than lives up to its name

Traditional dancing at Tjapukai Aboriginal Cultural Park

sand suitable for bike races, jogging or an afternoon or two of simple sunbathing. Just watch out for crocodiles. Once a little fishing village, Port Douglas has climbed on the tourism bandwagon, but it's more relaxed than Cairns. The fancy **Mirage Resort** is the flashiest hotel in town. Near it, Quicksilver runs catamaran services to the islands.

For practical purposes, the nearby sugar-milling town of **Mossman** is the end of the line for most people. From here northwards it's several hundred hot kilometres to the like-able river port of **Cooktown**, where Captain Cook's battered *Endeavour* was beached in 1770. The James Cook Memorial Museum tells all about it.

The tip of **Cape York Peninsula**, north of Cooktown, is a vast expanse of marshy terrain, prone to flooding and rife with crocodiles, only negotiable in well-equipped four-wheel-drive vehicles. The rivers are impassable from December to March; **Coen** is the last place for supplies and fuel.

NORTHERN TERRITORY

On the surface, the Northern Territory might seem an unpromising tourist destination. Its deserts, torrid tablelands and rainforests look immensely uninviting, and the region is especially discouraging when it's blazing hot. However, the wildlife is enchanting, the scenery is magnificent and the people, though few and far between, welcome the wandering stranger with Outback hospitality and charm.

The population of the self-governing territory totals only around 193,000. Their average age is 28 years, the youngest of any Australian state or territory. About one in five Territorians is an Aborigine, so cultural insights are part of the agenda for foreign visitors. This is the place to find the grandeur and mystery of the most sacred Aboriginal sites.

The Northern Territory covers about one-sixth of Australia's total area. Perhaps surprisingly, roads in 'NT' are generally of a high standard and a four-wheel-drive vehicle is not necessary unless you specifically want to pursue off-road activities. The climate effectively divides the land into two parts: the north, called 'the Top End', is lush and very hot. The rest of the Territory, known as 'the Centre', has drastically less rainfall. The Red Centre, with its infinite horizons and parched, rugged beauty, fits the stereotype of 'Back of Beyond'.

Darwin

Australia's northernmost port, the capital of the Northern Territory, is a young, prosperous city radiating the optimism of the reborn, for Darwin has survived far more than its share of catastrophes. At a cost of hundreds of lives, it was bombed scores of times in World War II. Rebuilt after the war, it was once again wiped out by a killer cyclone in 1974. Subsequently planners went back to the drawing board to design a bigger and better city. Darwin's deepwater port is being upgraded at a cost of about A$90 million to enhance the city's role as Australia's gateway to Asia.

The 85,000 Darwinians include more than 50 different ethnic groups, including a large Chinese community. This is reflected in the city's choice of Asian and Western eating-places, ranging from up-market restaurants to budget-priced food stalls at the **Mindil Beach Sunset Markets**, where seaside eating, shopping and entertainment combine.

Darwin's daytime temperature averages more than 30°C (86°F) virtually year-round. But while transients wilt, the locals know how to withstand the heat. They dress lightly and casually – even businesspeople wear shorts to work – they use air-conditioning and they drink a record amount of frosty beer to quench their thirst. Although elsewhere in Australia a stubby means a small beer, order one in Darwin and you get a two-litre bottle – almost half a gallon. This gives a clue to the Darwin sense of humour; and the jokes are nearly always a pleasant distraction from the heavy-handed heat. Empty beer cans often end up as the construction material for a flotilla of fanciful boats which compete in Darwin's annual slapstick regatta.

Local chauvinists will admit that Darwin, about 3,000km (1,860 miles) from Sydney and Perth, is 'a trifle isolated'. But that doesn't deter the eager newcomers arriving from all parts of the country – not least for such adventurous activities as bungee jumping, parachuting and bush walking.

City Sights

Historic buildings are the last things you'd expect to find in a city wiped out by a modern cyclone. But visitors can tour the restored 19th-century buildings that bring to mind the atmosphere of the pioneering days. Darwin's foundation as a permanent settlement dates back to 1839, relatively modern

Darwin's new Parliament House was opened in 1994

history even by Australian standards. The old **Government House**, overlooking the harbour, is an elegant example of colonial style (opened in 1883). Although a series of cyclones and the wartime bombs badly damaged the building (known as the Seven Gables), it has been put back together in fine form, and is surrounded by lovely tropical gardens. It replaced an earlier building which was eaten by termites. In turn, it has been replaced as the regional seat of government by a new **Parliament House**, opened in 1994.

Dating from 1885, the single-storey stone building known as **Brown's Mart** is now a theatre for live plays. The building has a checkered past. Built as a miner's exchange, it was converted for use as a police station and subsequently served the community as a brothel.

Also on an offbeat historical theme, the old **Fannie Bay Gaol** (open: daily 10am–5pm) was opened for business in 1883. Closed down in 1952, the jail is now a museum, where you can follow the advance of penal progress since those rough-and-ready days. The gruesome gallows were last used in 1952.

Other restored buildings include the **Victoria Hotel**, as Victorian as its name (built in 1894), and the former **Admiralty House**. A surviving portion of the old Anglican **Christ Church Cathedral** has been incorporated into the soaring modern building.

A relatively new tourist venue is the **Wharf Precinct**, housing **Indo-Pacific Marine** (live coral displays) and the **Australian Pearling Exhibition**; pearling has had a long history in the area, and the museum traces the industry from its beginnings.

The New Darwin

For the feel of modern Darwin, drift over to the **Smith Street Mall**, a pedestrians-only shopping area in the heart of the restored city. The shady mall, lined with stores, cafés and restaurants, is the perfect place for people-watching. All kinds of city and rural 'locals' congregate in the mall – there's even a walk-through fountain. If you want to take a photo, be forewarned: The 'Australian characters' who turn up here don't normally appreciate the attention.

The **Museum and Art Gallery of the Northern Territory** (open: Mon–Fri 9am–5pm, Sat–Sun 10am–5pm) at Fannie Bay is worth a visit for its Aboriginal art section and the exhibition commemorating Darwin's destruction by Cyclone Tracy on Christmas Eve 1974. It killed more than 50 people.

Another building that looks remarkably ambitious for a town of Darwin's size is the **casino**, a white pyramid of a leisure centre surrounding the magnet of gambling. Investors have a choice of traditional games in the sophisticated mould of Monte Carlo or the more folksy Australian style. You can try your hand at two-up, the Australian game that's as simple as tossing two coins. The excitement grips participant and hangers-on alike.

Lovers of tropical flowers will be delighted by every little garden around town, but the ultimate display occupies the **Botanic Gardens**, 34 hectares (84 acres) of the most fetching, fragrant flowers and plants. In addition to the bougainvillea

Darwin's futuristic casino

and frangipani, the orchids are a special source of pride.

Back to the seaside for something completely different: Doctors Gully, at the end of the Esplanade, is the site of a strange audience-participation ritual, the feeding of the fish. At **Aquascene**, tourists wade into the sea at high tide (check the local paper for the time) to hand-feed catfish, mullet, bream, milkfish and other sizeable denizens of the harbour. Thousands of fish turn up here daily for the festivities, returning to deep-sea pursuits until the next free handout.

Other cities are built around a central business district or a park, but Darwin stretches in all directions around its airport. This is handy for airline passengers but less so for the locals, who must go miles out of their way to get from one part of town to another if the two places happen to be on opposite sides of the runway.

On the north side of the airport near the Casuarina High School is a moving monument to the victims of Cyclone Tracy. It's in the form of a 'sculpture' of twisted iron girders, like roller coaster tracks gone wild. No artist produced this abstraction; it's merely the way three girders were contorted when the big wind destroyed a nearby building.

The devastation caused by Cyclone Tracy taught everyone a lesson in architecture and engineering. Now specially reinforced roof construction is required by law; houses should never again go sailing away. Even Darwin's **Chinese Temple**, notwithstanding its sweeping roofs, is guaranteed cyclone-proof. It serves Buddhists, Taoists and Confucians.

East of Darwin

In the tropical wilderness east of Darwin you can see natural phenomena known as '**magnetic anthills**', which are found scattered like prehistoric dolmens in the bush alongside the highway. To be accurate, these are neither magnetic nor anthills. They are termite mounds, the insect equivalent of skyscrapers, often taller than people, and are always aligned exactly north–south, for reasons unknown to scientists. They look like two-dimensional sandcastles.

Fogg Dam, 60km (37 miles) east of Darwin, is a splendid sanctuary for a dozen species of water bird coexisting on magical pools. This was the site of the Humpty Doo rice project, a multimillion-dollar scheme to grow rice without the disadvantages of the traditional feet-in-the-mud, aching-back method. According to the plan devised by the efficiency experts, aeroplanes effortlessly seeded the area in one fell swoop. Countless swarms of birds, not having been consulted, feasted on this manna from heaven as soon as the seeds hit the ground. Riceless, Humpty Doo had a great fall and went out of business. The area is again strictly for the birds.

Kakadu National Park

Birdwatchers, botanists and all other visitors are enthralled by **Kakadu National Park**, situated about 220km (135 miles) east of Darwin. The scenery ranges from romantic to awesome. As an unparalleled outdoor museum of ancient Aboriginal art, the park is on the World Heritage List of places of 'outstanding universal value' deserving protection. Timeless paintings on Kakadu's rock ledges are brimming with mystery and meaning. Some have remained here since the era of Europe's Paleolithic cave art.

Nineteen different clans of Aboriginal peoples live in the park's 6,144 sq km (2,372 sq miles), between the Wild Man and East Alligator rivers. They lease the land to the National Parks and Wildlife Service and participate in the park's management, including working as park rangers.

Nature has quite bluntly divided Kakadu into two worlds: the plains, with their

'Magnetic' termite mounds always point north–south

lagoons and creeks, and the escarpment, a stark sandstone wall marking the western edge of Arnhem Land. From the top of the high plateau waterfalls tumble to the lowlands in the wet season (November to March).

The floodplains entertain water birds by the thousand. Their names alone are enticing enough to turn laymen into dedicated birdwatchers: white-throated grasswren, white-lined honeyeater and white-breasted whistler, to list but three of the species that breed in the park. The star of the show, though, is the jabiru, a stately variety of stork.

In the mangroves you'll see striated heron, little kingfisher, broad-billed flycatcher and possibly also magpie goose, black shag, ibis and crested plover. A special delight is the sight of the delicately poised lotus bird, which seems miraculously to walk on the water.

The waterways are rich in the eminently edible barramundi. Less appetisingly, the estuaries are home to the saltwater crocodile, a vicious predator which preys on barramundi, birds, small animals and, sometimes, human beings.

Kakadu's Rock Art

At as many as a thousand different places in the park – most notably at Nourlangie and Ubirr rocks – ancient Australians left works of art, rock paintings in styles both primitive and eerily sophisticated. The earliest legacy consists of arrangements of handprints and the imprints of objects that were dyed and thrown at cliff walls and cave ceilings for decorative effect. Many centuries later, abstract-expressionist artists were to reinvent a similar splashy technique.

Ubirr Rock in Kakadu

The next generation of prehistoric artists concentrated on depicting the figures of animals. Among them is a curious variety of anteater believed to have become extinct perhaps 18,000 years ago, a valuable clue to the age of some of these paintings. The same school of artists painted stick-figure humans in hunting and battle scenes using ochre pigments for colour.

Later artists introduced movement into their pictures, such as hunters throwing spears or boomerangs. An innovation of this era was the use of abstract marks around certain figures, like a modern cartoonist's squiggles representing a character's surprise or fear.

NT's most fearsome predator: a 'saltie' or saltwater crocodile

A few thousand years after this, Aboriginal artists developed a remarkable style, now called X-ray painting. The profile of, say, a fish is clearly painted but instead of its covering of scales we see its bones and internal organs, with the emphasis on edible or otherwise useful parts.

After Australia was colonised, Europeans, too, became a subject for Aboriginal artists. There are pictures of the sailing ships the British arrived in and caricatures, scarcely flattering, of the new settlers holding recognisable muskets.

Katherine Gorge

The most spectacular natural attraction located at the Top End of the Northern Territory, **Katherine Gorge** is about 350km (217 miles) 'down the Track' from Darwin. The Track is what they call the highway linking the Timor Sea and Alice Springs in the Red Centre of Australia. Originally a rough path fit only for bullock carts and camel trains servicing the overland telegraph line, the route was upgraded by American servicemen in World War II to supply Darwin, which was dangerously isolated and under attack.

Kakadu's rock paintings feature stick figures in violent action

Katherine, to be precise, is not just a single gorge but a series of 13 gorges. In the wet season (from November to March) the torrents, waterfalls, whirlpools and rapids give an impression of thundering power. But it's uncomfortably hot and humid, and sometimes the rains cut off the roads. So **Katherine Gorge National Park** is best visited in the dry season (April to October), when the water flows at a relative trickle. Flat-bottomed boats cruise along the river, mostly on the lower two canyons, where the water reflects sheer cliff-sides, but more inquisitive travellers can explore the other 11 canyons upstream either by hiring a canoe or swimming. Walks and hikes offer other perspectives.

Among the sights are Aboriginal wall paintings portraying kangaroos and other native animals, bigger than life-size. Live kangaroos may be seen in the park, as well as the echidna (spiny anteater) and the dingo. Adding a tremor of excitement is the possibility of glimpsing a freshwater variety of crocodile called Johnstone's Crocodile. Unlike the 'salties' of the north, though, these fierce-looking reptiles are timid fish-eaters; fortunately, tourists do not figure on their menu. Bird life is colourful and includes hooded parrots and black cockatoos.

Alice Springs

Traffic lights have slightly tamed the adventurous Outback atmosphere of **Alice Springs**, the biggest town for a thousand miles around. 'The Alice' still looks rather like the frontier town you imagined: a relaxed, friendly, slightly dishevelled community of pioneers, dreamers, transients and, more recently, throngs of tourists.

The Northern Territory's second biggest population centre in the Red Centre has more than 26,000 inhabitants. When it comes to climate, they are extremists. In the summer it gets as hot as 42°C (108°F) but, mercifully, the nights in June, July, September and October require a sweater or two. Chances of seeing rain are slight. The Henley-on-Todd Regatta, a whimsical fixture each August, is run on the sandy bed of the sometime Todd River, a wide *wadi* gullying through the centre of town. The boats, of many classes, are all bottomless, and are hilariously propelled by the racing legs of their crews.

The Alice first grew around a waterhole discovered in 1871 by the surveying party stringing the first telegraph line from Adelaide to Darwin – and from there to the rest of the world. Alice Springs was named after Alice Todd, who was the wife of South Australia's postmaster general. He won himself a knighthood for pushing through the project; locally, the Todd River immortalises him.

Camels, traditionally ridden by experts from Afghanistan, brought the equipment for the telegraph relay station built at Alice Springs and the supplies to keep the technicians alive. When termites devoured the first telegraph poles, replacements – heavy iron poles brought in from Britain – also had to be transported by camel train. Telegrams aside, Alice Springs remained isolated until World War II – and until the 1960s it was little more than a crossroads market town. Now it's thriving as a staging post for tourist jaunts throughout the Red Centre.

Like many an Australian town, The Alice is bigger than you might expect, but the essentials can be taken in on a walking tour. In the main street, **Todd Street**, is the **John Flynn Memorial Museum**, dedicated to the founder of the flying doctor service, and **Adelaide House** (open: Mar–Nov, Mon–Fri 10am–4pm, Sat 10am–noon), the first hospital, which is now a museum. In nearby Parsons Street is the **Old Stuart Town Gaol** (open: Mar–Dec, Mon–Fri 10am–12.30pm, Sat 9.30am–noon), dating from the beginning of the 20th century, complete with 'his' and 'hers' dormitory cells.

The **Royal Flying Doctor Service** (guided tours Mon–Sat 9am–4pm, Sun 1–4pm), which brings health care to the furthest cattle ranch, began in Alice Springs in 1928. You can visit the base, on the south side of town. Another service which eased development of the Outback, the **School of Distance Education** (open: Mon–Sat 8.30am–4.30pm, Sun 2.30–4.30pm), a radio link with isolated pupils, has its headquarters on Head Street.

A couple of kilometres (just over a mile) north of town, an unspoiled park surrounds the restored **Telegraph Station** (open: daily May–Sept 8am–7pm; Oct–Apr 8am–9pm). This was the most important relay station on the line. Before the wires were strung a message could take three months to reach London from Adelaide. The relics here give a glimpse of 19th-century technology and the lonely life of the telegraph pioneers.

> **The Aboriginal Land Act of 1976 returned about one-third of the Northern Territory to Aboriginal ownership. You need a permit to enter many Aborigine-controlled areas, but not to drive through them on a public road.**

South of The Alice on the Ross Highway is a **camel farm**, offering rides atop swaying beasts, the descendants of the camels that supplied the pioneers. It also houses snakes and lizards in the **Arid Australia Reptiles Display**. In July each year, the local Lions Club sponsors the Camel Cup – an exciting day of camel races at Blatherskite Park. The animals are launched from a kneeling start in a cloud of dust, and run just as fast as racehorses, though rather less gracefully.

The old Telegraph Station at Alice Springs

The **Todd Tavern** at the top of Todd Mall is the town's liveliest drinking spot. There's also an 'international standard' casino, **Lasseters**, on Barrett Drive. Enthusiasts have a choice of blackjack, roulette and a sophisticated version of the Australian game of two-up *(see page 141)*, along with the excitement of poker machines and keno, a game resembling bingo.

An eccentric enterprise on Petrick Road southeast of town, desert winery **Chateau Hornsby** (open: Mon–Sat 9am–5pm, Sun 9am–9pm, closed Dec–Jan) produces 1,000 cases of wine a year. Here, in 'Australia's farthest winery from anywhere', wines grow in coarse red sand under a fierce sun. They need to be watered daily. The resulting wines, with quaint names such as Horny Tawny, may be sampled on the spot.

Alice Springs Desert Park (open: daily 7.30am–6pm), which has gained worldwide recognition for its achievements in breeding rare and endangered species, is located about 3km (2 miles) out of town along Larapinta Drive. A visit starts with a 20-minute film, then you tour walk-through enclosures and see the desert animals. It's instructive and entertaining.

Racing for the Camel Cup at Blatherskite Park, Alice Springs

A popular excursion from The Alice concentrates on **Standley Chasm**, 50km (31 miles) to the west. This passage through the MacDonnell Ranges dwindles to the narrowest gap. The walls are so high and steep that the sun penetrates the bottom only fleetingly at midday. A few slender trees bravely sprout from the rockface high above, reflected in the cool, still water of a natural pool at the far end of the gorge. In the wet season, from November to March, rainwater can suddenly flood the chasm.

The recently paved **Mereenie Loop Road** links Alice Springs with the remote desert points of **Kings Canyon** and **Yulara**, the latter being the site of Uluru (Ayers Rock). The loop forms a dedicated tourism drive called **Pioneer's Path**, which heads through the western MacDonnell Ranges on its way into Alice Springs. The trip covers about 1,200km (750 miles) and takes between three and five days, giving an incredible Outback experience on the way.

Uluru (Ayers Rock)

As the sun begins to sink beyond the rim of the desert, the crowds with their cameras gather by car and bus along 'Sunset Strip', the tongue-in-cheek name for a dusty stretch of car park. As the onlookers watch **Uluru (Ayers Rock)** undergo its striking changes of colour, they are not solemn but rather festive, friendly and relaxed. By coming here, they are fulfilling an Australian dream, getting to know this mystical 500-million-year-old rock that rises up from the red heart of the country.

The world's greatest rock, seemingly dropped by divine design in the middle of nowhere, actually protrudes from a buried mountain range. At 348m (1,142ft) tall and some 8km (5 miles) around, it is even more impressive than the dimensions suggest. Standing alone in a landscape as flat as a floor, and tinted as bright as in your imagination, the monolith certainly lives up to its reputation. You'll need no complicated explanations to understand why the Aborigines consider it sacred.

The Aborigines have owned the rock under Australian law only since 1985 – Uluru is the Aboriginal name; the small local Aboriginal community leases it back to the government for use as a national park in return for a healthy income, as well as participation in its management.

For the Aborigines it's not just a rock, it's a vital aspect of Dreamtime, encompassing the creation of the earth, linked with the life of the present and future. Various parts of the monolith are designated as sacred sites; they are signposted, fenced off and barred to outsiders.

The most inspiring views of the rock are to be seen at dawn and dusk. It's well worth getting up at six in the morning to stake out the mighty silhouette from 20km (12 miles) away, waiting for the sunrise. As first light strikes the lonely monolith it appears to catch fire, glowing red, then orange, finally

Uluru (Ayers Rock) is the tip of a buried mountain range

seeming to emit rays of wondrous power. Only then the desert world comes to life: a hawk squawks, a rabbit rustles the brush, and hordes of pesky flies begin to buzz. (Waving your hand in front of your face soon becomes second nature in the Outback, like a horse flicking its tail. Insect repellent helps, too, but the flies seem to outnumber the people 20 to one. Maybe this is why Aboriginal legends mention bothersome flies.)

If you're fit you can join the crowds climbing the rock, although local Anangu Aboriginal people regard this as disrespectful. A few hours are enough for the return trip via the marked trail, which has a protective chain you can grab when the going gets too steep or windy. The ascent requires no mountain-climbing experience or equipment, but do wear sensible rubber-soled shoes and carry drinking water. From ground-level the climbers reaching the summit look like a line of very tired ants. Some climbers die during the experience; they are commemorated by plaques placed discreetly on the base of the rock. The plaques reveal causes of death to be generally heart-attack among older climbers and fatal plunges by younger ones.

Another worthwhile (and safer) way to get to know the rock is to join a walking tour led by a park ranger, circum-

navigating the base. Up close, the monolith discloses its var-
iegated surface, with its caves, dry rivulets, furrows, wounds
and gashes, and what might be taken for fanciful engravings
60m (200ft) tall. Alternatively you can take a 20-minute
flight from Alice Springs to view the rock and its surroundings from the air.

Only 36km (22 miles) by road west of Ayers Rock, and visible from its summit, is another stupendous rock formation,
the **Olgas** (Kata Tjuta). From afar, Mt Olga and its satellites
look like a scattering of dinosaur eggs or sleeping elephants,
but they're even higher than Ayers Rock. Here, too, dawn and
dusk colour the most fascinating views, the fantasy shapes

changing with the hues and the movement of the shadows. You can get to know the Olgas by a choice of hiking routes. The popular trail from the Kata Tjuta car park up to the look-out is officially called 'suitable for family enjoyment', but it's steep and tricky enough to deter both the very youngest and oldest generations.

The Yulara Development

To cope with hundreds of thousands of visitors each year at Ayers Rock, a comprehensive resort has been built. It could have been a disastrous blot on the landscape, but the **Yulara Ayers Rock Resort** fits in benignly, 20km (12 miles) from the rock. The complex is almost entirely camouflaged, and too low-slung to detract from the majesty of the surroundings.

The facilities start with sites for tents and caravans, and go up to a five-star hotel with gardens, pool, spa, restaurants and bars, television and in-house video; and, of course, air-conditioning. It makes for quite a change after a day spent slogging through the desert. The visitors' centre in the hotel and shopping complex offers information, literature and audiovisual shows explaining the desert, the wildlife, geology, mythology and other angles to enhance your appreciation of the Red Centre.

Several airlines serve Yulara, and the views of the desert on the way are spellbinding. Otherwise you can take a bus or drive; it's about 450km (280 miles) by paved road from Alice Springs, a whole day in which to become acquainted with the desert in its many forms – flat and desolate or covered with scrub, thinly forested or, more rarely, sand undulating in post-card-worthy dunes.

The best time of year to visit is between May and October, when the days are sunny and warm and the nights refreshingly chill. In January, by contrast, the mean maximum temperature is 36.6°C (98°F) – not quite conducive to hiking.

The red road to Kata Tjuta: the name means 'many heads'

Surviving the Outback

Three-quarters of Australian land is desert – 'burning wastes of barren soil and sand', as the poet Henry Lawson described it. These vast empty spaces on the map hold an irresistible challenge for intrepid adventurers. Only vaguely comparable with desert of the Sahara type, the far Outback supports vegetation – sometimes even luxuriant – and fascinating wildlife. If you do want to venture off the surfaced roads and explore the unknown, there are a few precautions you must take.

• Do not even consider driving into the Outback in the summer; the heat is unbearable. In the 1840s, explorer Charles Sturt recorded temperatures of 69°C (157°F) in the open and 56°C (132°F) in the shade. It was hot enough to melt the lead in his pencil and force screws out of wooden boxes. Just think what it could do to your car!

• Rain can also be a source of disaster; after many years of drought, it can suddenly pour down for an entire week, and

The Yulara Ayers Rock Resort can accommodate 5,000 visitors a day

the land is transformed into an enormous flood plain. So make sure you never camp in a dry riverbed.

• Your vehicle should be a reliable four-wheel-drive, with a complete set of spare parts: two spare tyres and tyre repair kit, two spare tubes, coil, condenser, fan belt, radiator hoses and distributor points, a tin of radiator leak fixative, spark plugs, an extra jack (with a large baseplate to prevent sinking in sand or mud), 5 litres (a gallon) of engine oil, a pump, a tool-kit, an axe and a small shovel. Keep the petrol tank full and carry at least 20 litres (5 gal) in reserve.

• You will need reliable maps and be sure to plan your route in detail – and stick to the plan relentlessly. At your point of departure, advise the police of your route, the estimated time of arrival at your destination, and the amount of rations you are carrying. Report to the police again when you arrive. Always seek local advice about the hazards you may encounter. If you wish to enter Aboriginal lands, you must first obtain permission from the Aboriginal landowners, and at least four weeks' notice is required. Inquire at the government tourist office for the appropriate address. In some areas you have to be equipped with a two-way radio.

• Take adequate supplies. Most important is water – you will need 6 litres (1½gal) per person per day, best carried in metal containers. Emergency rations should be made up of high-energy foods such as dried fruit, with canned meats, soup and fruit drinks. Some invaluable components of your first-aid kit will be aspirin, water-purifying tablets, salt tablets, diarrhoea pills, insect repellent, disinfectant, bandages and sun-block. Your personal survival kit, which you should carry with you at all times, must contain a compass, map, whistle, waterproof matches, pocket knife, bandage and adhesive plaster.

• Other essentials: a set of billycans (pails or pots with lids and wire bails), several sheets of heavy-duty plastic (2m/6ft square) and a length of rubber or plastic tubing. A piece of nylon rope (30m/100ft long) may also be useful.

• Wear loose, light cotton clothing and cover your head. Space blankets can prove a boon: the shiny aluminum side turned towards the sun reflects heat away from the body, keeping the temperature normal. To keep warm, turn the shiny side inwards.

• Do not drive at night. Kangaroos are a real hazard, and you may collide with wild water buffalo, attracted to the roads at night because the surface is warmer than the ground itself.

In Case of Catastrophe

If your car breaks down, above all do not panic. Stay with your vehicle; it will be a welcome source of shade, and it is more easily spotted by aircraft than a person on their own.

• Make visible distress signals, using brightly coloured clothing or any available material – anything that contrasts with the earth.

• Move around as little as possible, to conserve your body fluid. All your physical exertion should take place during the cool night hours.

Heading into the Outback

• Your main preoccupation must be water. It is important to ration your supply and set about collecting more by making a solar still, as follows: dig a hole about 1m (3ft) square and 50cm (20in) deep, away from any shade. Place a large billycan (pail or pot) in the bottom of the hole, and surround it with leafy foliage. Then cover the hole with a sheet of plastic and seal the edges completely with earth, making sure that the plastic does not touch the interior walls of the hole. If you have a length of rubber or plastic tubing, place it in the bottom of the billycan before you seal the edges of the sheeting, leaving the other end outside to act as a siphon. Place a small stone in the centre of the plastic sheet, right over the billycan. Moisture from the ground will condense on the underside of the plastic sheet and will drip slowly into the billycan. In this way you will collect about 2 litres (½ gal) of water per hole per day, so it's best to make several stills, at least 3m (about 10ft) apart. You will need to change the position of the still every three to four days.

• Small animals – frogs, lizards and snakes – are attracted to the stills and may provide an extra source of food. In principle, anything that walks, crawls, swims, flies or grows from the soil is edible – or so they say. But beware of anything that has a bitter taste and of plants with a milky sap.

• Another source of food and water in the northwest of Australia is the bottle-tree, which preserves water in its hollow trunk for months after the wet season has ended. In an emergency you can also eat the rind of bottle-tree pods, chopped up and stirred with water – it's nourishing but certainly not gourmet fare.

The prospects may seem harrowing, but after all, the Aboriginals have survived and even thrived in this forbidding land for at least 50,000 years.

WESTERN AUSTRALIA

When it comes to elbow room, the state of Western Australia has no competition. It's bigger than Texas and Alaska combined and more than ten times the area of Great Britain.

Most of the state's vast expanse is desert, semi-desert or otherwise difficult terrain. The bulk of the population of about 1,860,000 has therefore gravitated to the Mediterranean climate found around the beautiful capital city of Perth. Closer to Jakarta than to Sydney, Perth faces the Indian Ocean with an open, outward-looking stance. Here the cares of the big population centres of eastern Australia seem worlds away.

The state's Outback produces great wealth, and even the forbidding deserts are bursting with minerals. It was gold that brought the state's first bonanza, during the 1880s and 1890s, followed by nickel, bauxite and iron. Considerably more appealing are the above-ground riches: the hardwood forests, the orchards and the vineyards. And, since the climate is so sunny, it's only fair that there is a beach for every possible mood along the 6,400km (4,000 miles) of coastline.

The startling, but harmless, frill-necked lizard

The first European to set eyes on a Western Australian beach (in 1616) was Dirk Hartog, a Dutch navigator making his way from the Cape of Good Hope to Java. It was not long before other Dutch travellers touched base here, and one of them reported spotting a wallaby, though not by name; he thought it was a giant cat with a pouch for its kitten. Later in the 17th century, the British adventurer William Dampier happened upon Shark Bay, near Carnarvon, and could hardly wait to leave: the land seemed hopeless for farming, there was no drinking water, and he dismissed the indigenous population as 'brutes'.

More than 200 years after Hartog's discovery of Western Australia, the British finally got around to colonising it. The site chosen, on the Swan River, became Perth. But what the Colonial Office considered a good idea turned out to be less brilliant in practice. It would take more than the scenery and the climate to attract settlers to what seemed, even by Australian standards, the end of the world. Problems of development persisted, including poor communica-

---

From Coast to Coast

It takes just 4½ hours to fly from the South Pacific to the Indian Ocean, from Sydney to Perth, but if you have 65 hours to spare, you can make the journey by train. The Indian-Pacific, a luxurious but not particularly rapid train, crosses the country twice a week in each direction. On its 3,955-km (2,457-mile) journey, it crosses the Nullabor Plain, with one section that's the world's longest stretch of straight track – 479km (298 miles) without a bend. There are numerous stops, but few towns, and none of any importance. In fact, there's not much to see – nothing but scrub, blue sky and telegraph poles for days on end – but passengers are well catered for with an observation lounge, a bar and even a music room, complete with piano.

tions, financial difficulties and a shortage of workers. Prospects for the new frontier became so precarious that the colony's leaders had to make an appeal to London, asking the government to send over a supply of forced labourers – convicts.

Even so, nothing really worked in Western Australia until the gold rush during the 1890s, when the population quadrupled in

Black swans are as noisy as they are handsome

just ten years. Throughout the 20th century, the discovery of mineral deposits throughout the state provided the main basis of its wealth – from uranium to gas and oil on the northwest shelf. Once it was launched on the road to prosperity, there was no stopping Australia's largest state. Its isolation finally ended in the early years of the 20th century, when the transcontinental railway linked Perth and Sydney. Western Australia reached new heights of self-confidence and fame in 1983, when the yacht *Australia II* wrested the America's Cup from the US there, for the first time ever.

Perth

Bright new high-rise office buildings scrape the clear blue skies of Perth. If this city brimming with vigour and enthusiasm were a person, you might imagine it had been born with the proverbial silver spoon in its mouth: a handsome, clean-cut youngster with every possible advantage, inevitably growing up to become an unqualified success in life.

Although history refutes the silver-spoon theory, you can't miss Perth's easy self-confidence. The people are relaxed, friendly and anxious to help the stranger. They are proud of their efficient town and its up-to-date facilities – the stylish shopping arcades, the art galleries and Entertainment Centre – and the great sailing, swimming, surfing and fishing right on its doorstep. The inhabitants won't fail to inform you that this tidy city sprawling magnificently along the looping river is Australia's sunniest state capital.

Sunshine aside, Perth has called itself 'the city of lights' since the early days of the American manned space programme. As John Glenn, the first American to orbit the earth, passed over the city, middle-of-the-night Perth switched on every light bulb in town. It was a friendly gesture that brightened the lone astronaut's flight and put Perth's name in lights.

Perth's skyscrapers are crowded around the Swan River

City Sights

Few will get a chance to enjoy a spaceman's perspective, but the view over Perth from **King's Park** is a good compromise for sizing up the city below. These 400 hectares (990 acres) of natural woodland and wild flowers, manicured lawns and picnic sites, solemn monuments and lively playgrounds are found on the top of a bluff called **Mt Eliza**, right on the edge of the city centre. From here you look down on the wide Swan River as it meanders toward the sea, on the business district with its gleaming skyscrapers, and on the complexity of the well-landscaped municipal freeway system.

The **Swan River** was named after the indigenous black swans found here, first noted with amazement by the 17th-century Dutch navigator Willem de Vlaming. Unlike swans in the Northern Hemisphere, which are white and prone to whistling or grunting when they are not naturally mute, the black swans sound off like a band of clarinets noisily tuning up. They're such tame creatures that they'll take bread out of the palm of your hand without biting.

The Swan River begins about 240km (150 miles) inland in the wheatlands of Western Australia. For most of its long journey, under the name of Avon River, it is only seasonally navigable, and occasionally downright treacherous. But here, with the Indian Ocean close enough to salt it, the Swan widens into a lake, and invites reflection – and attracts flotillas of breezy yachts. By the riverside in the centre of town, the **Old Courthouse** really is old, especially by local standards. Built in Georgian style in 1836, it's the oldest public building in Perth.

Stirling Gardens, surrounding the courthouse, is a restful hideaway. The 'Ore Obelisk' monument here looks like a giant shish-kebab impaling all of the minerals mined in Western Australia; but don't expect to find gold or diamonds on the skewer – they don't seem to count.

The **Town Hall**, at the corner of Hay and Barrack Streets, was built in the 1860s by convict labour. If you look closely at the outline of the windows of the tower, you may perceive the design of broad arrows – the prison symbol that was stencilled on convict uniforms. Similarly Tudor in inspiration, but even less of an antique than the Town Hall, **London Court** is a 1930s shopping mall done up in touristy 16th-century style, leaded windows and all. It fits in quite happily with the modern stores and interconnecting shopping precincts radiating from the **Hay Street Mall**, the main shopping street of Perth. Cars are prohibited here, so the window-shopping is very relaxed. The mall is usually animated by a melange of street entertainers – musicians, magicians, jugglers or mimes.

A couple of blocks north, across Murray Street Mall, is **Forrest Place** on the corner of Wellington Street. Here, in Albert Facey House, you'll find the Perth Visitor Centre (tel: 1300 361 351) – an abundant source of brochures, maps, tickets, tours and bright ideas, all cheerfully dispensed by the helpful staff.

In a city as young as Perth, with its skyline of tall, modern office buildings, those historic structures which have escaped the developer's demolition ball are proudly pointed out to visitors. **Government House**, found on the main street, St George's Terrace, is the official residence of the Western Australia governor. Its Gothic effects date from the 1860s. Built by hard-working convicts, the house is used nowadays for a variety of state occasions and as a place to accommodate visitng VIPs.

The elegant terrace leads directly to the **Barracks Archway**, the last vestige of a headquarters building of the 1860s. This crenellated three-storey structure has been preserved as a memorial to the early colonists. Behind the brick archway you can catch a glimpse of the **Parliament House**, where the state legislature holds forth.

On the other side of the railway tracks – you can cross the unusual Horseshoe Bridge by foot or car – stands the **Old Gaol**, which was constructed and used by convicts in 1856. Nowadays, the jail forms part of the **Western Australia Museum** (open: daily 9.30am–5pm). The museum offers rather more than penal relics of the wild-west days – there is also an extensive collection of Aboriginal rock paintings, head-dresses and weapons, and a 10-tonne meteorite. The nearby **Western Australia Art Gallery** (open: daily 10am–5pm) displays paintings from several continents.

Perth's Town Hall holds its own among the city's high-rises

Also north of the city centre is the **Northbridge** district, which is full of lively ethnic restaurants, pubs and nightclubs, especially around James and Lake streets. If you're in the mood for gambling, head for the **Burswood Casino**, near the Causeway Bridge. Here, under one roof, you'll find more than 140 gaming tables, plus a cabaret, restaurants and bars.

Back in the centre of town, you can hardly miss the **Entertainment Centre** on Wellington Street. Not quite Perth's answer to the Sydney Opera House, this roundhouse landmark can pack in as many as 8,000 fans for rock concerts or ballet. Another cultural focus in this area is the Concert Hall, the headquarters of the state's symphony orchestra. If you're looking for stage plays, the most atmospheric house is **His Majesty's Theatre**, now restored to its sumptuous Edwardian standard.

The **Aquarium of Western Australia** (open: daily 10am–5pm), an underwater-tunnel aquarium with interactive displays, offers whale-watching trips in season. For action entertainment, experience thrill rides at **Adventure World Theme Park** (open: Sept–Apr daily, 10am–5pm). Nearby, daredevils can try their hand at bungee-jumping from a 12-m (40-ft) tower, or parasail to see the sights of the city from a higher perspective.

To the Coast

It's only 19km (12 miles) down the river from Perth to the capital's Indian Ocean port, **Fremantle** – an enjoyable outing on one of the cruise boats that ply the Swan River. The river tours begin in the centre of Perth, at the **Barrack Street Jetty**. On the south side of the **Narrows Bridge**, note the **Old Mill**, built in 1835, an imposing white windmill in the Dutch style from the first half of the 19th century. Perfectly restored, it's open for visits 10am–4pm.

Beyond this, on the opposite shore, spreads what looks like another transplant from Europe. The campus of the **University of Western Australia** was constructed and landscaped in a Mediterranean style, from the shrubs right up to the orange-tiled roofs.

Matilda Bay harbours only a relative handful of the swarms of sailing boats that call the Swan River home. During World War II this was a base for Catalina flying boats. The bay is the site of the Royal Perth Yacht Club, where the America's Cup was treasured behind bulletproof glass from 1983 until it was lost to the United States in 1987.

The coastline of the Dalkeith district, near **Point Resolution**, is called Millionaires' Row. The view of these fine mansions from the perspective of the river might evoke a dash of envy; even millionaires from out of town could become jealous at the sheer opulence of these homes.

Freshwater Bay was named by the crew of HMS *Beagle*, the survey ship made famous as the vehicle for Charles Darwin's researches into natural selection. Beyond this bay, and a zigzag, the river tapers to a fairly narrow-gauge artery spanned by two bridges. Long-suffering convict labour built the first bridge at this site in 1866. It proved a boon to one of its creators, a celebrated outlaw named Moondyne Joe, an escape artist. The night before the ribbon-cutting ceremony, he broke out of Fremantle Prison and gave himself the honour of becoming the first, if unofficial, pedestrian to cross the bridge over the Swan River. He made a clean getaway.

Matilda Bay is the home of the Royal Perth Yacht Club

Fremantle

Although it's a serious international port, you'll remember the city of Fremantle for its casual charms. A Mediterranean-style sunniness combines with a Victorian quaintness to give Fremantle its special character. The town may be cosmopolitan, but it is also as down-to-earth as its classic examples of convict architecture.

For many years Fremantle – 'Freo' to the Aussies – lay becalmed, a long way from the big time of tourism. Then came the America's Cup saga and a sudden saturation of world attention. New-found pride inspired the townsfolk in their sparkling campaign to restore the old terraced houses and other relics in time for the 1986–87 defence of the Cup. At the same time, the marina facilities were also vastly expanded and improved.

Whether you think of Fremantle as a yachting base or a workaday port, you'll want to see the sights of the harbour. There is a mixture of dream yachts, trawlers, ocean liners and cargo ships of every stripe.

Fremantle's highest point is **Monument Hill** in **War Memorial Park**. There are three memorials altogether, including one for the US personnel based in Fremantle who died in World War II. Another, an original periscope, commemorates the British and Allied submarine crews who perished in the same conflict. This is the place to watch the sun set over the Indian Ocean.

Back near the waterfront, and wasting an enviable view, the 12-sided **Round House** (open: daily 9am–6pm) looks like the forbidding, windowless prison it used to be. Actually it's much more cheerful from the inside, with its sunny courtyard. Constructed in 1831, the Round House specialised in the lesser criminals, although it was the site of the state's first hanging; generally, incorrigibles were shipped off to the rigours of Tasmania.

The **Western Australian Maritime Museum** (open: daily 10.30am–5pm) was built by convicts to house the Commissariat, the bureaucracy in charge of them. Here's a chance to see some notable shipwrecks, most notably the wooden hull of the 544-tonne (600-ton) *Batavia*, the flagship of the Dutch East India Company, which went aground in 1629 and was salvaged and restored in the late 20th century.

The **Fremantle History Museum** (open: Sun–Fri 10.30am–4.30pm, Sat 1–7pm), at the other end of town, occupies yet another convict-built complex which has had an interesting career. It first served as a lunatic asylum for deranged prisoners, then as a training centre for midwives, later as a home for elderly women, and in World War II it found new life as a headquarters of the US Navy. Now demobilised and brightly restored, the Colonial Gothic building houses exhibits on the history of Fremantle and its people.

An ancient anchor outside the Western Australian Maritime Museum

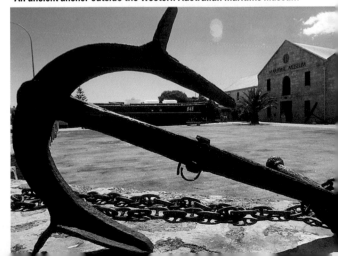

If you're visiting Fremantle at the weekend, check out the lively **markets** on the corner of Henderson Street and South Terrace, from 10 or 11am to 5pm.

Rottnest Island

Don't be put off by the name: there is nothing rotten in the state of Western Australia, and certainly not on Rottnest Island. Even in the original Dutch, the name does the island no justice. Apparently Commodore Willem de Vlaming, who landed here in 1696, confused the indigenous quokkas (a species of small wallaby) with some imaginary species of rat. So he called the island Rottnest, or rat's nest. In spite of this unkind mistake, the Dutch explorer considered Rottnest an earthly paradise. You may well agree.

The Rottnest Hotel, popularly known as the Quokka Arms, was built in 1864 and originally served as the summer residence of the governor of Western Australia.

A good reason for going over the sea to Rottnest (18km/11 miles from Fremantle) is to see the fetching little quokkas, with babies in their pouches, like their kangaroo cousins. Other attractions are peacocks and pheasants, which were introduced when the governors of Western Australia used the island as a summer residence. And you can spot dozens of other species of birds, including the curlew sandpiper, the red-necked stint and the osprey. Since 1941 the island has been a wildlife sanctuary, where it's forbidden to tamper with any of nature, even the snakes.

Rottnest is as quiet as an idyllic, barefoot sort of isle ought to be. The number of cars is severely limited. Bicycles are the most popular way of exploring the 40km (25 miles) of coastline. Look into the swimming, snorkelling, fishing and boating opportunities.

Four ferry operators serve Rottnest Island (nicknamed 'Rotto' by Aussies) from Perth or Fremantle. It's an 80-minute cruise from Perth and double that from Fremantle. You can fly there in 20 minutes.

De Vlaming thought this quokka's ancestor was a rat

Excursions Inland

Just to the east of Perth, the **Darling Range** is the beginning of the great inland plateau. Amid the tall trees and colourful wildflowers are lookout points with superb views of the city and the sea. Waterfalls, brooks and dams refresh the relaxing scene.

At Wooroloo in the Darling Range is **El Caballo Blanco** (The White Horse), a Spanish-style ranch and Lippizana horse stud, where the magnificent Andalusian horses are trained in the Spanish style, and give daily demonstrations of their dressage prowess.

The **Swan Valley**, only about half an hour's drive northeast of Perth, is a high-priority destination for wine-lovers. The area is noted for its small, family-run vineyards. The wine-making tradition in the Swan Valley dates back to the foundation of Western Australia. If wine-tasting and driving seem incompatible, you can take a coach tour of selected vineyards, or the even more popular river cruise with stops at one or two wine-cellars.

Further east, the 150-km (90-mile) green expanse of the **Avon Valley** provides pastureland for cattle and grows the grain to feed Perth and beyond. The colony's first inland settlement, **York** is proud of its history. More than a dozen

The Swan Valley is full of small, family-run vineyards

19th-century buildings, including an extravagantly designed Town Hall, have been restored; several now serve as museums. Just outside town, one of the early farms has been restored to a 'living museum' in which you can watch blacksmiths and wheelwrights at work. Clydesdale horses still plough the fields.

The nearest national park to Perth, **Yanchep** is known for its eucalyptus forests, its wild flowers and a series of limestone caves. There is also an island-studded lake called **Loch McNess**, named after a local philanthropist, Sir Charles McNess. Don't bother looking for a Loch McNess monster. You can, however, see a koala colony here.

Natural Wonders

A spectacle reckoned to be more than 2.5 billion years old is **Wave Rock** – one of those natural phenomena worth a long detour. And it will probably require one – it's a 700-km (437-

mile) round trip by road from Perth. The rock stands near the small town of **Hyden**, about 350km (220 miles) inland from Perth, in the wide-open spaces where the wheat, oats and barley grow. The rock itself takes the form of a stupendous surfer's wave, as tall as a five-storey building, eternally on the verge of breaking. Walking under the impending splash is one of the state's most popular tourist activities. Energetic visitors can also climb to the top. Other extraordinary rock formations in the area have expressive names like Hippo's Yawn and The Humps.

In **Nambung National Park**, about 250km (155 miles) north of Perth, the **Pinnacles Desert** is notable for myriad limestone pillars jutting like stalagmites from the desert floor. Standing as high as 5–6m (16–20ft), the Pinnacles are scattered over perhaps 400 hectares (1,000 acres). The imagination runs wild. When Dutch explorers first sighted the Pinnacles from their vessels, they thought they had found the ruins of a long-deserted city. In fact, they are entirely natural. Limestone formed around the roots of plants growing on stable dunes about 30,000 years ago. The plants died and the dunes moved on, leaving the calcified structures exposed. The park entrance is located near the lobster-fishing village of Cervantes.

The Southwest

Excursions to the southwestern corner of the state encompass a delightful variety of scenery: beaches, vineyards, orchards and soaring **jarrah forests**. Where the water table is high, you'll see stands of paperbark trees; you could strip off a layer of the papyrus-style bark and write a letter. But the most impressive tree in the region is the jarrah, a giant variety of eucalyptus. The lower half grows straight and clean as a tele-phone pole, with all the branches emerging at the top.

Less than 10 percent of Western Australia's original old-growth forests are still standing, but the state's Labour government, which came to power in February 2001, has pledged to protect all of it from logging to safeguard the future of eco-tourism in the state. So the forests will still be there when you arrive.

Bunbury is a pleasant vacation town in the southwest, and you can swim with the amazingly tame dolphins at Koombana beach there. The **Margaret River** region, an area found between Cape Naturaliste and Cape Leeuwin, is honeycombed with limestone caves, some of which are open to the public. South of Dunsborough, **Yallingup Caves** form a fantastic underground world of elaborately carved limestone. Check with the local tourist office for details of how to gain access.

The bizarre limestone spires of the Pinnacles

Margaret River lies at the heart of the state's top wine-growing and gourmet dining region. Specialities include brie, fresh berries and marron (freshwater shellfish), while accommodation ranges from boutique guest-houses to five-star hotels or camp-sites under a million stars. Enchanting little places to stay include Cape Lodge, built in South African Cape style. Relaxing yet elegant, this is the perfect location from which to tour noted vineyards, including Cape Clairault, Leeuwin Estate, Cape Mentella, Sandalford and Vasse Felix.

The Goldfields

Kalgoorlie, located about 550km (340 miles) east of Perth, retains the atmosphere of the riotous gold-rush town it was in the 1890s. The streets, laid out in a grid, are wide enough for stagecoaches or camel trains to make a U-turn. It's like a Wild West movie set, and there are verandahed saloons for every occasion. Optimists still scan old worked-over sites in search of forgotten nuggets – and the occasional whopper still turns up.

The first big strike of Kalgoorlie gold came in June 1893, when an Irishman named Patrick Hannan stumbled onto enough glitter to really kick up a fuss. Paddy Hannan has never been forgotten in Kalgoorlie. A bronze statue of the bearded prospector has a place of honour in the main street, which bears his name; a replica of the water bag he carried serves as the municipal water fountain.

When Hannan's news spread, the almost total lack of water was the first desperate hardship to face the thousands of prospectors who rushed headlong into the goldfields. Disease and death from dehydration took a heavy toll. The solution was found by another Irishman, an engineer named C.Y. O'Connor who constructed a 560-km (350-mile) pipeline from a reservoir near Perth. You can still see the big above-ground pipes by the side of the road. Wounded by criticism of the project, O'Connor killed himself before the first drop of water reached Kalgoorlie; he is now honoured by a statue on the waterfront in Fremantle.

As the prospectors came in from the surrounding desert with their sudden wealth, Kalgoorlie turned into a rip-roaring supplier of wine, women and song. The pubs were legion; many still retain their frontier atmosphere. Another old mining tradition is the red-light district of Hay Street, although at last inspection only three of the notorious 'tin-shack' brothels were still in business. You can gauge how prosperous the

Old gold workings in Kalgoorlie

town was from the elegance of the Victorian buildings, most notably in the three-storey arcaded headquarters of the **Museum of the Goldfields** (open: daily 10am–4.30pm). This institution is stacked with exhibits detailing the life and work of those early prospectors.

As for gambling, the town doesn't have a casino, but 7km (4½ miles) out in the country on the Menzies Road 'Australia's only legalised bush two-up school' flourishes from midday to sundown. Just follow signs marked 'Two Up'.

Hannan's North Tourist Mine (open: daily 9am–5pm) is a former mine converted for tourism use. You can take a 40-minute journey underground. Ex-miners conduct the guided tours and they are most interesting – although most people are delighted to see daylight again.

A ramshackle train called the Rattler (for obvious reasons) makes a one-hour loop around Kalgoorlie's Golden Mile twice daily, departing **Boulder** station at 10am and 12.45pm. Boulder, by the way, is Kalgoorlie's neighbouring (and slightly shabbier) twin town.

A year before Paddy Hannan's big strike at Kalgoorlie, gold was discovered at **Coolgardie**, 40km (25 miles) to the west. Today Coolgardie proudly bears the slogan of 'ghost town'. In fact, ghosting is its principal industry, and if there's a bit of melancholy in the air, it can only be good for business. The historical markers here seem to far outnumber the population, which at the turn of the 20th century was 15,000 and now stands at about 2,000. Any good ghost town needs an interesting cemetery, and the inscriptions on the headstones in Coolgardie's graveyard tell revealing stories of the harsh frontier life. Among the Afghan camel drivers buried here, at least one is listed as having been murdered.

The Kimberley

More than 1,500km (930 miles) north of the gold lode, one of the richest diamond mines in the world gives a sparkle to the rugged and remote **Kimberley** region of Western Australia.

The **Argyle mine** produces a sizeable heap of exquisite pink diamonds – a coveted rarity in the gem world – as well as vast quantities of industrial diamonds that are used for grinding and drilling. Machines beside which humans look like tiny Lilliputians move the ore along to the Argyle processing plant, where millions of glittering carats are then yielded per year .

You must be aged 18 to be admitted to the Kalgoorie two-up school, outside of town. A serious tourist attraction, the arena looks something like a bear-baiting pit. The rules of the game, which was invented by convicts, are ludicrously simple. One player tosses two coins in the air, trying to make them both come down heads. The other players bet on his chances of success.

The Kimberley, a dramatic, elemental and spectacular area of waterfalls, thunderstorms, searing heat and torrential rain (the latter two depending on season), is thought to hide as many as half of all the diamonds on earth. But that's not its only distinction.

More than three times the size of England, the Kimberley has fewer people per square kilometre than almost anywhere else in the world. Generations of isolation have left the Kimberley the most Aboriginal part of Australia, with some

30 percent of land tribal and half the population black. The enormous region is particularly known for Aboriginal rock art, including the mysterious '**Bradshaw figures**', named after explorer Joseph Bradshaw, the first European to describe them. In 1891, Bradshaw wrote: 'The most remarkable fact in connection with these drawings is that wherever a profile face is shown, the features are of a most pronounced aquiline type, quite different from those of any native we encountered. Indeed, looking at some of the groups, one might almost think himself viewing the painted walls of an Egyptian temple.' The drawings are believed by scholars to have derived from an unknown culture that flourished some time before 15,000 BC – long before the Egyptians had built their temples.

Until a few decades ago, the Kimberley was the domain of intrepid explorers. It has been opened up since, with tour operators using four-wheel-drive vehicles, boats, helicopters and small aircraft to reach far-flung attractions: towering gorges on the Fitzroy River; **Purnululu (Bungle Bungle) National Park** with its orange-and-black beehive-striped mounds; the sandstone and volcanic country of **Prince Regent Nature Reserve**; the tidal 'waterfalls' near Derby; and the eerie **Wolfe Creek Crater Meteorite Reserve**. The meteorite crater is 850m (930yds) across, with a rim 50m (165ft) high. Aborigines call the area *Kandimalal*, which means 'the place where the snake emerged from the ground'. Europeans only discovered it in 1947.

Coastal Attractions

On the coast, the seaport of **Broome** has a romantic past. It once supplied 80 percent of all the world's mother-of-pearl. Divers from Japan, Malaya and the Philippines went out on 400 boats, diving for oysters and the pearls within them. The Asian aura still lingers, even though the mother-of-pearl business died with the introduction of cultured pearls and plastic buttons. You will find evidence of past glories in **Chinatown**, in the old Japanese boarding houses, and in the gambling and other pleasure palaces – all reminders of the port's early 20th-century heyday.

The main attraction today is **Cable Beach**, a fantastic 22-km (14-mile) stretch of golden sands, so named when the underwater communication link between Broome and Java (and so on to London) was established in the 19th century. At **Gantheaume Point**, low tide exposes dinosaur footprints about 130 million years old. If you stay late on the beach in March–April or August–September you may be lucky enough to see a natural phenomenon called 'the Staircase to the Moon', an illusion caused by the full moon reflecting on mud flats. It can be seen from the jetty at extreme low tides.

The extraordinary Bungle Bungles in Purnululu National Park

SOUTH AUSTRALIA

The state's official animal symbol is the hairy-nosed wombat, but don't let that put you off. This shy native of South Australia is just as cuddly as any koala (but rather heavier); it is merely lacking the services of any public relations advisers to polish up its image.

Like the amiable wombat, South Australia is self-reliant. Everything the state needs can be found within its borders: coal from the open-cut mines of Leigh Creek, gas under the northeastern desert, grain and cattle through hundreds of miles of latitude, fish from the

Dinosaur footprints at low tide at Gantheaume Point *(see page 143)*

Southern Ocean, and world-renowned wines from scenic vineyards. South Australia produces more than 70 percent of Australia's wine.

The sights of South Australia are as many and varied as its resources: with the rugged grandeur of the Flinders Ranges, the sand dunes of the north, the green banks of the Murray River, and the surf of the Great Australian Bight.

The history of South Australia is distinctive. Nothing quite so gross as convict settlers here; the colony was founded as a planned community run by wealthy idealists. The 'free settlers only' tag is a source of local pride. Sobriety and morality were keystones of the master plan, giving rise to a reputation for stuffy puritanism. Fortunately, the influence of the state's 'wowsers' (killjoys) has long faded. For example, Maslin's Beach just outside Adelaide became Australia's first legal nudist beach *(see page 156)*.

In some social respects, South Australia has led the rest of the country. It was first to grant votes to women, first to appoint an Aboriginal governor and first to appoint a woman governor. Spread across 1 million sq.km (390,000 sq miles), the state occupies one-eighth of the entire continent. But because most of the state is unendurable desert, the inhabitants number only about one-twelfth of Australia's total population. And most of these may be found living contentedly in the graceful capital city.

Adelaide

Adelaide is easy to reach. Its international airport is efficient, land transport links are good and the city offers a cheerful introduction to Australia. Adelaide's sunny climate beams on the city's many parks and gardens, as well as its elegant squares and broad boulevards.

With a population of just over one million, Adelaide is a relatively sophisticated capital, where culture and good living are important elements of the local scene. There is a significant art gallery and the world's largest collection of Aboriginal artefacts in the South Australian Museum. Every other year (even-numbered years) the city puts on a world-acclaimed international festival of the arts and a concurrent fringe festival. In the intervening, odd-numbered years, you can enjoy Womadelaide in February, a music festival with indigenous musicians from around the world.

Every day, the locals here pay tribute to international culinary art, dining out in hundreds of excellent restaurants. Chefs work with top quality raw material. You can see and taste it at the **Central Market** in Gouger Street – fresh produce

South Australia's mascot

from all parts of the state, including McLaren Vale olives, Coffin Bay oysters, Barossa mettwursts and Riverland dried fruits.

Nightlife encompasses concerts, clubs, strip shows and a casino. The city has come a long way since the days when outsiders joked, 'I went to Adelaide once but it was closed.'

Adelaide was founded two generations after the settlement of Sydney, in the reign of King William IV, and named after his queen, the former Princess Adelaide of Saxe-Meiningen. Although the southern coastline had been well charted, the idea of building a city beside the Torrens River didn't catch on until the 1830s. Before the first earth was turned, the city was planned on paper, street by street and park by park. The business district covers the area of precisely one square mile (2.6 sq km). The model, with its built-in green belt, was a winner, and so it remains.

City Sights

The most stately of streets in Adelaide, a considerable superlative here, is **North Terrace**, which delineates the northern edge of the business district. North Terrace is lined with trees and distinguished buildings – mansions and museums, churches and memorials. Between the Terrace and the gently sloping, landscaped bank of the river is the **Adelaide Festival Centre**, which calls to mind Sydney's Opera House, but with angular planes in place of billowing curves; Adelaide also managed to truncate Sydney's lavish price tag. The relatively budget-priced $20-million complex has a theatre for every occasion. The 2,000-seat Festival Theatre (Australia's largest) is convertible, in three hours, from an opera house to a concert hall with outstanding acoustics. A drama theatre seats some 600 people, an experimental theatre 350.

There are hourly backstage tours of the establishment and a theatre museum preserves South Australia's rich history and interest in the performing arts. Outside, bold sculptures are strewn around the plaza. You can eat outdoors in the Festival Centre bistro overlooking the river, or make your own picnic on the lawn. Or take a sightseeing boat up the river to the **zoo** (open: daily 9.30am–5pm), where you can pet the kangaroos and admire an outstanding collection of Australian birds.

Just behind the Festival Centre, the **South Australian Parliament House** (guided tours daily 10am–2pm) is dignified by ten Corinthian columns and so much expensive stonework it earned the nickname of the 'marble palace' . The foundation was laid in 1881 but work continued, on and off, over the following 58 years. Next door, the **Constitutional Museum**

Festival Frenzy

Sydney, Melbourne and Perth may all have their arts festivals, but none compares in size, prestige or sheer excitement to Adelaide's. Few cities in the world have such an extraordinary range of performance spaces, from the gleaming white Festival Centre to the outdoor amphitheatres and intimate lofts. The 'official' festival lures the high-profile international acts, kicking off with free weekend concerts and firework displays in Rundle Park. At the same time, the fringe festival, for lesser-known performers and artists, attracts literally thousands of acts from all over Australia, Europe and North America. Every spare corner of indoor space is devoted to some art exhibition, and every stretch outdoors to a site-specific installation. By any standards, it's a remarkable happening.

The dramatic white Adelaide Festival Centre stands in Elder Park

(open: Mon–Fri 10am–5pm, Sat–Sun noon–5pm) occupies the former Legislative Council building. It's Australia's only museum of political history. Just across the road is **Government House**, the official residence of the Governor of South Australia.

A startling change of pace lies in ambush just next door: **Adelaide Casino** (open: until 4am, 24 hours at weekends) is situated in a dazzling conversion of the vastly domed old railway station. They've created a wonderfully plush gambling den which, with its potted palms, marble floors and mighty chandeliers, is open to the public. The visitors seem to prefer keno, a bingoesque game, to the complexities of blackjack, roulette, baccarat and the other international pastimes offered.

Elsewhere along North Terrace, the **University of Adelaide** is at the heart of a cluster of cultural institutions. Whale skeletons fill the show windows of the **South Australian**

Museum (open: daily 10am–5pm) as an alluring invitation. Inside is a monumental collection of Aboriginal artefacts. A striking large-screen video display relates the story of the Aboriginal Dreamtime hero Ngurunderi. Other countries are well represented in a comprehensive survey of ceremonial masks, shields and sculptures from South Pacific islands. And you can see a traditional trading vessel from New Guinea, which remained in service until recent times, with a bamboo deck and a sail made of bark. The museum also features a didactic display of stuffed Australian animals, reptiles, birds and fish.

The **Art Gallery of South Australia** (open: daily 10am–5pm), which officially opened in 1881 and reopened in 1996 after a $20-million makeover, covers many centuries of the world's art, ranging from ancient Chinese ceramics to contemporary Australian prints, drawings, paintings and sculptures. The gallery is also home to an extensive collection of Aboriginal art.

Two more historic buildings on North Terrace are **Holy Trinity Church**, the first Anglican church built in South Australia (begun in 1838), and **Ayers House** (open: Tues–Fri 10am–4pm, Sat–Sun 1–4pm), a 45-room mansion furnished in an opulent 19th-century style. The house was owned by a local businessman and statesman, Sir Henry Ayers, after whom an admiring explorer named Ayers Rock. He was premier of South Australia seven times, and used Ayers House for state functions. Its ballroom, the hub of the Adelaide social scene, was regularly washed down with milk to make the floor fast and smooth.

To the north of Ayers House lie the **Botanic Gardens**, 20 hectares (50 acres) of lawns, trees, shrubs and lakes, with some exceptional botanical buildings as well, from the old Palm House brought from Germany in 1871 to the extraordinary Bicentennial Conservatory of 1988.

Parallel with North Terrace is **Rundle Mall**, an all-weather pedestrian mall, and the heart of Adelaide's shopping area. Its trademark is a sculpture comprising double-decked spheres of stainless steel reflecting the animation all around. The mall's merchants include department stores, boutiques, cafés and restaurants, all enlivened by street entertainers. The **Myer Centre** includes the city's two best department stores (along with a futuristic amusement area called Dazzleland), and Rundle Mall contains Adelaide's two best pubs, the Exeter and the Austral. Rundle Street (the eastern extension of Rundle Mall) is an arty and pleasant quarter. The westward extension of Rundle Mall, Hindley Street, has clubs, live entertainment, amusement arcades and strip joints.

Located on Grenfell Street is **Tandanya** (open: daily 10am–5pm), an Aboriginal cultural centre offering art galleries, a workshop and performing arts. The shop there is a good place to buy authentic Aboriginal souvenirs.

North of the city centre, **Light's Vision** is not a sound-and-light show, as its name may suggest. It's a monument to the foresight of Lt-Col William Light, who was sent out in 1836 to find the ideal site for a model city, then devise the total plan for its development. Atop a pedestal on Montefiore Hill, his statue peers over the parklands, pointing at the city of Adelaide, which he created.

Nearby Places

Adelaide has an outstanding public transport system, including the highly efficient O-Bahn, a 'bullet bus' that steers itself along its own smooth roadway at speeds of up to 100 kph (over 60 mph). It's billed as the fastest suburban bus service in the world. But nostalgia persists: the last surviving tramcars still clatter along between the edge of Victoria Square and the seashore at suburban **Glenelg**. This old-fashioned beach resort, from which a fishing pier forges far out to sea, was the original landing-place of the colonists who founded South Australia. A full-size replica of their vessel, a converted freighter named HMS *Buffalo*, moored nearby, is now a museum and restaurant. Among other beaches near Adelaide, from north to south along the Gulf of St Vincent, you will find Semaphore, Grange, Henley Beach, West Beach, Somerton, Brighton and Seacliff.

To the south and east of the city, the **Adelaide Hills**, the last manifestation of the Flinders Ranges, provide a background of forests, orchards and vineyards. There are pleasant walks,

William Light contemplates his city from the top of his pedestal

lovely walks, fine views, and plenty of picnic possibilities. The highest of the hills, Mt Lofty (770m/2,525ft) is only half an hour out of town by car. You can look down on the hang-gliding enthusiasts riding the hot air currents on the leisurely route back to sea level.

Hahndorf, a hill village situated approximately 30km (19 miles) southeast of Adelaide, has changed little since it was settled in 1839 by German refugees. To the delight of sightseers, many of the original buildings in this oldest surviving German settlement in Australia have been restored. A number of folklore events brighten the tourist calendar, especially the Founders Day Festival, a marksmanship and beer-drinking celebration every January, and St Nicholas Night in December.

Up the River

▶ When it comes to the **Murray River**, Australians seem to go into rapturous delight. Having few rivers, they are thrilled by the local equivalent of the Mississippi. The Murray begins life in the Snowy Mountains (the Australian Alps), becomes the frontier between Victoria and New South Wales, and enjoys its last meandering through the state of South Australia. It is the river that accounts for the beautiful vineyards, orchards and pastures along the way, not to mention the boating, fishing and waterskiing. In the 19th century the river was a main thoroughfare for both passengers and cargo, but the advent of railways and highways left the Murray more of a pleasure route.

Paddle steamers churn up nostalgia along the lower Murray, only an hour's drive from Adelaide. A variety of boats – big and small, ultramodern and old-fashioned – offer short excursions or voyages of several days. It's also possible to hire a houseboat and ply the river at your own pace, in which case you can fish for your own dinner. The Murray cod run to gargantuan sizes, and you can vary your diet by catching 'yabbies', big freshwater crustaceans akin to crayfish.

The Barossa Valley

▶ Australia's best-known wine-producing region, the **Barossa Valley**, is also the prettiest. The scenery is a touchingly beautiful landscape of soft hills, sheep-grazing land, cosy villages, and the rows of vines that produce some famous wines. The Barossa's 45 wineries produce about a quarter of Australia's total vintage. The valley is easy to explore: just 30km (19 miles) long by 14km (9 miles) wide. Accommodation ranges from luxurious colonial mansions (with dinner, bed and breakfast) to historic settlers' and miners' cottages, small motels and fully serviced caravan and tent sites.

Barossa was founded by Germans who arrived in 1842 fleeing religious persecution at home. The Germanic atmosphere became a real liability when Australia plunged into World War I. Some of the Teutonic place names were changed for 'patriotic' reasons, and the government shut down a German printing house for fear that it would produce subversive leaflets.

Nowadays, the Germanic atmosphere pervading the valley is all part of the charm. You'll see neat stone cottages with filigreed verandahs and decorous gardens; if the inhabitants came out wearing lederhosen it wouldn't be much of a shock. You'll get to taste *Bratwurst* and *Sauerkraut* to the accompaniment of oom-pah music.

The Barossa Valley is only about an hour's drive northeast of Adelaide, a perfect distance for an easy all-day excursion

The sun sets over the ranks of Barossa Valley vines

devoted to sniffing out the local colour and sampling the wines. Many of the wineries here are geared to this transient trade, advertising guided tours of the premises and offering explanatory tastings. Be warned that the vineyard route is so popular that the roads and cellars can get crowded on Sundays and bank holidays.

Every other year (the odd numbers) the Barossa Valley stages an ebullient Vintage Festival in March or April, a week-long carnival as earthy as the wines it celebrates. The locals – and thousands of visitors from Australia and overseas – dance in the streets, sing, play games, eat and do a fair amount of drinking.

Barossa produces about a quarter of all Australia's wine

Kangaroo Island

South Australia's favourite escapist resort, Kangaroo Island is so big that you could spend a week finding the best places for swimming, fishing and sightseeing. Approximately 145km (90 miles) long and 30km (19 miles) wide, it's the country's third largest island, after Tasmania and the Northern Territory's Melville Island. For tourists in a typical rush, though, there are one-day excursions; it's only half an hour by air from Adelaide.

The explorer Matthew Flinders, who circumnavigated Australia at the beginning of the 19th century, chanced upon Kangaroo Island in a storm. His hungry crew, amazed to be met by a mob of fearless, friendly kangaroos, consigned some of the reception committee to the stew pot. Grateful for the sustenance, the great navigator named the place Kangaroo Island. Right behind the Flinders expedition came a French explorer, Nicolas Baudin. Despite having lost the territorial claim to the British, he contributed some French names to the island's features. They're still on the map: places such as D'Estrees Bay, Cape Du Couëdic and Cape D'Estaing. Later settlers acknowledged Baudin's effort and built a white-domed monument to him at Hog Bay, called **Frenchman's Rock**.

The capital of Kangaroo Island, **Kingscote**, has a permanent population of around 1,450. Its elongated pier is where the car ferry from Port Adelaide docks, and the island's airfield is only a few kilometres inland. Dolphins and seals can be seen frolicking just offshore.

In 1919 the western end of the island was designated a nature reserve. **Flinders Chase National Park** is South Australia's biggest. Technically this is not a zoo; the animals are in their natural state, but in the absence of predators the kangaroos, koalas and emus have become extroverts, trying to sponge or steal some food from the visitors.

On the south coast, **Seal Bay** belongs to Australian sealions. They are so unafraid of humans that you can wander among them at will, except in certain fenced-off areas. Birdwatchers thrill to local species, which show clear differences from mainland relatives, and a noisy population of migratory birds from distant oceans.

Three Peninsulas

Just to the south of Adelaide, the **Fleurieu Peninsula** is an easy-to-reach, easy-to-like vacationland of surfing beaches, vineyards and history. The history starts at the beginning of the 19th century when the French explorer Baudin named the peninsula after his navy minister, Count Pierre de Fleurieu. The first industry to be based on the peninsula was whaling, centred on **Victor Harbour**. It's now the area's biggest town, and a very popular year-round resort.

Yet another historic location is **Maslin's Beach** on the Gulf St Vincent coast. Here a new leaf was turned in the evolution of Australian social customs. This was the nation's first legal nudist beach. Now there are many to be found around the coastline.

Further inland, scores of vineyards basking in the sunshine of the Southern Vales are the reason for the peninsula's fame. They've been making wine here since 1838, to great effect. Many of the wineries encourage connoisseurs or simply wine drinkers to stop in and try the vintages. The best-known area of wine production is **McLaren Vale**.

Why 'Kangaroo'?

According to legend, Captain James Cook asked an Aborigine what that strange leaping animal was. 'Kangaroo', came the reply. Cook immediately passed on this intelligence to the whole world. Much later, it was established that the word *kangaroo* meant 'I don't know' in an Aborigine language. There are around 45 species of kangaroos and wallabies in Australia, ranging in size from the red kangaroo, taller than a man, to the musky rat kangaroo, about the size of a guinea-pig. Members of the family have adapted to a range of habitats: open plains, woodlands, rocky outcrops and cliffs – and some even climb trees. A young kangaroo, born in a near-embryonic state, crawls into its mother's pouch and attaches itself to a teat. It will continue to develop there for another four to eight months, depending on the species. Even when it is capable of venturing out and feeding itself, it returns to the safety of the pouch between expeditions.

The **Yorke Peninsula**, located west of Adelaide, first became important during the 19th century as a copper-mining district. The majority of the region's miners were drafted in from copper-rich Cornwall in England, and the Cornish touch can still be seen in the design of the old cottages and churches in the area. Museums and the ruins of the mine superstructures provide constant reminders of the peninsula's heyday, which continued until the

Australian sealions in Seal Bay

1920s. They've even kept up the homely tradition of baking Cornish pastries.

The **Eyre Peninsula** encompasses beach resorts, wheat fields, bushland, industrial centres and a prized wilderness, the **Lincoln National Park**. Set atop magnificent cliffs at the tip of the peninsula, the park is home to kangaroos and birds as diverse as emus, parrots and sea eagles. Fishing boats big and small are anchored in the attractive deepwater harbour of **Port Lincoln**, the tuna-fishing capital of Australia. Visit the home of the great white shark on a cruise to Dangerous Reef.

Port Lincoln celebrates **Tunarama Free Festival** on the foreshore of Boston Bay each January over Australia Day weekend (26 January). Highlights include the World Record John West Tuna Tossing Championship, which sees world-class athletes turn up to throw large fish. The current record was set in 1998 by Sean Carlin, who won gold for Australia in the hammer throw at the 1996 Atlanta Olympics, before switching to fish. Carlin hurled a tuna 37.23m (122ft), leaving awe-struck onlookers gasping.

The biggest city on the peninsula is **Whyalla**, which grew from a solid base of heavy industry – as heavy as iron and steel. If a blast furnace is your idea of fun, you can join one of the tours of the local steelworks (Mon, Wed and Sat at 9.30am); you can also visit the iron-mining area.

The Eyre Peninsula reaches as far west as **Ceduna**, where the vast expanse of the **Nullarbor Plain** begins. It's more than 1,200km (745 miles) from Ceduna westward to the next town of any significance (Norseman, WA). Filling stations do occur, but the route is lonely and gruelling. Nullarbor is sometimes thought of as an Aboriginal word. It's actually Latin for 'treeless', an indication that the plain is also waterless. But, as the Aboriginal inhabitants have always been aware, water is there if you know where to look for it: underground in limestone caverns. The highway follows the dunes and cliffs that lie along the length of the Great Australian Bight, which forms the bulk of the continent's curving southern coast.

The Flinders Ranges

For scenic splendour, South Australia's Outback competes well with the remote areas of the other states, nowhere more impressively than in the **Flinders Ranges**, 450km (280 miles) due north of Adelaide. Rising from a landscape as flat as the sea, the tinted peaks speak poetry to lovers of robust scenery. In the spring the rugged wooded hillsides come to life with a flood of wildflowers, but at any time of year the scene is intriguing. The mountains, like the desert, are much more colourful at close range.

An outstanding phenomenon found in the Flinders Ranges is a huge natural basin called **Wilpena Pound**. Rimmed by

Colourful vegetation at Wilpena Pound in the Flinders Ranges

sheer cliffs, the saucer is approximately 20km (12 miles) long and 8km (5 miles) wide. Although it looks like a crater, it was actually formed by folding rocks. Wilpena Pound is not only spectacular as a scenic and a geological curiosity, it also wins admiring squawks from the birdwatchers. This is a place where you can spot species including butcherbirds, wagtails, galahs, honeyeaters and wedge-tailed eagles.

The flat floor of the Pound is perfectly designed for bush walks (suggested routes are signposted) – but not in summer, when it's altogether too hot for unnecessary exertion. In any season it's essential to carry a supply of drinking water. There's only one way into the amphitheatre, through a narrow gorge occupied in rainy times by Wilpena Creek.

An area of such grandeur was bound to inspire Aboriginal myths and art over thousands of years. Timeless rock paintings can be inspected near Wilpena at Arkaroo and at Yourambulla, south of the village of Hawker.

Coober Pedy

The opal-mining town of **Coober Pedy** must rate as one of the most bizarre tourist attractions in the world. When you say 'desert' this is what it means: in the summer the daytime temperature can reach 50°C (122°F). That's in the shade, of which supplies are extremely limited. In the winter the nights become unpleasantly cold. Yet a couple of thousand people make their home in this far corner of the Outback.

At first glance, the town looks like a hard-hit battlefield. The almost treeless terrain consists of hundreds of mounds of upturned earth. But beneath the surface, things are not so bleak. The name Coober Pedy comes from an Aboriginal phrase meaning 'white fellow's hole in the ground' for the settlers have survived here by burrowing hobbit-like into the side of a low hill. The temperatures within are constant and comfortable, regardless of the excesses outside. Among the dugouts are residences of some luxury, with electricity and wall-to-wall carpets. Also underground are a Roman Catholic chapel, a bank and an air-conditioned motel.

Regular tours by bus or plane bring the curious crowds to Coober Pedy, which is about 950km (590 miles) northwest of Adelaide. The tours visit the local opal fields, where most of the world's opals are mined, with demonstrations of opal cutting and polishing. Having learned the intricacies, you can buy finished stones and jewellery on the spot. Or try noodling in the mullock heaps: all you need is a rake or a sieve to sift through the rubble at the top of each mineshaft, and if you're lucky you may find an overlooked opal. But note that amateur fortune-seekers need a permit (obtainable from the Mines Department in Coober Pedy or Adelaide) to go fossicking.

Opal is not a crystal but more like quartz, made up of silica with a small amount of water. Unlike diamonds, opals are used only for jewellery.

VICTORIA

By Australian standards, the state of Victoria is a midget. About the same size as Great Britain, it is the smallest state on the mainland. But its nearly 4.8 million inhabitants give Victoria Australia's highest population density.

Opals can be white, yellow, red, blue or black

Two out of three Victorians live in the capital, Melbourne, a centre for finance, industry, culture and sport. The sophisticated city folk live within easy striking distance of the state's bushland and 19th-century boomtowns, the sea, the vineyards and the ski slopes. Some of the scenery is so rich and pretty that the state's first name was Australia Felix – Latin for bountiful or lucky.

Victoria was the earliest state to industrialise, but it's still a leading farming power as well – hence the nickname of 'Garden State'. This agricultural potential remained unexploited until the 1860s, after the state's gold rush fizzled out. Unemployed ex-prospectors eagerly fanned out as farmers, working land they bought for £1 per acre. Immigrants in search of a figurative pot of gold followed in a steady flow that reached a tidal wave after World War II, with the policy of 'populate or perish'. This produced both curious ethnic pockets around the state and the cosmopolitan effervescence of a multicultural society within the dignified confines of the capital city.

Melbourne

Elegant parks and gardens splash green patterns across Melbourne's map, softening the rigours of its precise grid plan, and offering merciful breathing space on the edges of the city centre's hubbub. This is a friendly city of serious buildings and imposing Victorian architecture. Its air of distinction may have something to do with the fact that the city was founded not by prisoners (as was Sydney) but by adventurous free enterprisers with their own vision of success.

It's all so grand you might forget Melbourne's rough-and-tumble pioneering days. The gold rush broke out in Victoria in 1851, only a few months after the fever hit New South Wales. A gold strike at Ballarat so electrified the state that Melbourne itself risked becoming a ghost town; businessmen locked their offices or shops and rushed to the goldfields, and ships were abandoned by their gold-crazed crews. New immigrants rushing in to fill the gap lived in shacks and tents. Successful diggers, on their return to Melbourne, had so much money to dispose of that morals loosened considerably.

The long-running rivalry between Sydney and Melbourne is incurable. Fans of Sydney thinks Melbourne is boring, while those of Melbourne think Sydney is superficial. Sydneysiders blast Melbourne's climate; Melburnians ridicule Sydney's self-satisfaction. Generally, Melbourne (with a total population of about 3.5 million) seems to be on the defensive, for instance on the subject of the unpredictable weather; temperatures are subject to extremes. And as for Sydney's Opera House, Melbourne was determined to outdo it, but in a 'warm and welcoming' way, avoiding what was pointedly called 'self-conscious grandeur'. The outcome was the Victorian Arts Centre, a promising security blanket for local self-confidence.

If Melbourne is staid, as Sydneysiders allege, you'd never know it from their sports mania. 'Footy' – or Australian Rules Football – is the main attraction here. Cricket is also a passion. And as for the horses, the Melbourne Cup is so all-engrossing that the first Tuesday in November, when the race is run, counts as a legal holiday.

In the last couple of decades of the 20th century, Melbourne was a city that emptied after dark, but all that has changed dramatically. Residents have moved back into the inner city, and the Central Business District now has cafés, bars and nightclubs. Melburnians have something of a reputation as gourmets, and would not dream of deciding which of the 3,000 or so restaurants to patronise until they have diligently compared them in the local epicure guidebooks.

City Sights

A pleasant aspect of Melbourne can be viewed from the level of the Yarra, the river embellishing the centre of the city. On the last few miles of its journey to the sea, the Yarra plays host to freighters, pleasure boats and rowing regattas. And it waters the gardens, reflects the skyscrapers and invites cyclists and joggers to follow its course along pretty land-

Sophisticated Melbourne, also a main financial and commercial centre scaped paths. For a look up at the skyline and a close-up of river commerce, take one of the cruise boats that leave from **Princes Walk** by **Princes Bridge**.

Aerial views over the river and the city point up the ample acres of green (contrasting with yellow and russet leaves in autumn) in the parks and gardens in among the business-like blocks. The best vantage point is the observation deck on level 55 of Australia's tallest building, **Rialto Towers** on Collins Street. The view extends beyond Westgate Bridge to the west, the Dandenong Ranges to the east and the shimmering expanse of Port Phillip Bay to the south. The observation deck, with a licensed café bar, stands 253m (830ft) high. A 143-seat theatre called Rialto Vision shows a 20-minute film.

Melbourne: elegant 19th-century buildings amid the skyscrapers

An inescapable sight along the waterfront is the enormous **Crown Entertainment Complex**, housing the 500-room Crown Towers Hotel and Crown Casino. The casino, Australia's largest gaming establishment, offers (at last count) 350 gaming tables and 2,500 video gaming machines. The complex also houses an enormous spa covering an entire floor, decorated in a style one observer compared to 'a set from a Charlton Heston Bible epic'.

Southbank, a riverside shopping and strolling precinct, runs alongside. On the opposite bank is the *Polly Woodside*, a square-rigged sailing barque, recalling the adventurous days of the last century. Launched in Ireland in 1885, the restored ship is now part of a maritime museum.

Near the river, just south of the heart of town, an Eiffel Tower-style superstructure marks the modern **Victorian Arts Centre**. This airy silver, gold and white spire rises from flowing curves suggesting a ballet dancer's tutu.

The first part of the complex to open, in 1968, was the **National Gallery of Victoria** (open: daily 10am–5pm), now a high-priority stop for art lovers from the world over. The big collection includes European and Asian art, old and new, and of course offers a comprehensive look at Australian painting and sculpture. Among the choicest items on show are a vast, anecdotal Tiepolo painting from the 1740s, *The Banquet of Cleopatra*; sculptures by Rodin, Henry Moore and Barbara Hepworth; a first-class survey of classical Chinese porcelain; and a splendid sampling of Australian Aboriginal paintings. The Gallery, founded in 1861, is the oldest such institution in the country. In comfortable modern surroundings it hits its stride with the wealth of Australian paintings from the 18th century to living masters. And remember to tilt your head back to admire the immense, 10,000-piece stained-glass ceiling of the Great Hall.

The **Theatres Building**, directly beneath the symbolic spire identifying the Arts Centre, is the place to see opera, ballet and musicals. Under the same roof are a playhouse for drama and a smaller studio theatre for performances of more intimate works. The adjoining **Concert Hall**, which seats 2,700 people, is used for symphony concerts, but the acoustics can be changed to suit other types of performance. If you're not going to a concert, nip in for a glance at the artwork in the lobby, or take a guided backstage tour. The complex provides dining opportunities from snack bars to luxury-class restaurants.

Just across Princes Bridge on the north side of the river, the spires of **St Paul's Cathedral** are not as old as they look. They were added in the 1920s, several decades after the original Gothic-style structure was completed. The church is a refreshing hideaway in the midst of the busiest part of the business district, a few steps away from the Victorian mass of the main railway station and a less obvious historic landmark, **Young and Jackson's** pub. In the bar upstairs hangs a notorious oil painting of the nude 'Chloe', which has delighted many generations of beer drinkers since it scandalised Melbourne's art exhibition of 1880. By today's standards, it's quite staid.

Just north of St Paul's Cathedral in the new **Federation Square**, along with various recreational amenities, is the **Ian Potter Centre** (open: daily 10am–5pm), a stunning new gallery dedicated to contemporary Australian art. Federation

It could have been Batmania

Australia's second city could have had a rather foolish or embarrassing name if the Governor of New South Wales, Sir Richard Bourke, had not been a traditionalist. The first settlement of tents and huts on the Yarra had been called Bearbrass, for reasons that are not entirely clear. Yarra Yarra was also suggested as a possible name for the growing town, and so was Batmania, in honour of J. Batman, a settler from Tasmania who bought 40,000 hectares (100,000 acres) from the Aborigines. (The fact that he bought the territory, albeit at a derisory price, rather than simply stealing it, was a rare occurrence for the period.) But when Bourke visited the region in 1837, he decreed that the town should be named, in the customary fashion, after a British dignitary – in this case the Prime Minister, Lord Melbourne.

Square, which replaces the former City Square, has been designed to become Melbourne's primary recreational and cultural space.

The **Town Hall**, on the opposite side of Collins Street, was built in the 1860s. It is used for concerts and official happenings, and can hold 3,000 people.

Collins Street and the parallel Bourke Street are the reason Melburnians claim to have the best shopping in Australia. Three great department stores – Myer, David Jones and Daimaru –

Trams have right of way on Melbourne's streets

are located conveniently close together, surrounded by small trendy shops, and a warren of arcades for making the most of those rainy hours. The outstanding example of an old-time Melbourne shopping institution, the glass-roofed **Block Arcade** is an 1892 copy of a Milan landmark, the Vittorio Emmanuele Galleria. The **Bourke Street Mall** is a pleasure to roam. Diversions are provided by clowns, magicians, bagpipers and other entertainers. But don't get carried away by the relaxed atmosphere: although this is a pedestrians-only zone, there is one big exception – the trams rattle right down the middle of the mall.

By way of historic buildings, Melbourne likes to show off **Parliament House**, set in its own park facing Spring Street. It has been called the finest legislative headquarters this side of London; in fact, many of the furnishings found here are copies of those in Britain's Palace of Westminster. The federal government used this as its temporary headquarters in Australia's early days. The building, which dates from 1854, is open for guided tours when the state parliament is not sitting.

Older than any of the city's well-preserved Victorian buildings is **Captain Cook's Cottage** in Fitzroy Gardens. The great discoverer never lived in Melbourne; the stone house was transplanted in 1934 from Great Ayton in Cook's native Yorkshire (now Cleveland). In truth, it would be more accurate to call it Cook's parents' cottage, since there is no evidence that the good captain did live under its tiled roof in his 18th-century childhood. The only genuine Cook relic in the place is a small sea chest with the initials J.C.

Only in Australia, it seems, are jails such popular tourist attractions. The most fascinating of all is the **Old Melbourne Gaol** (open: daily 9.30am–4.30pm), situated just across the street from the modern Police Headquarters on Russell Street.

Parliament House, once the seat of Australian government

Opened in 1854, the three-storey penitentiary was the scene of more than 100 hangings. The death masks of the most famous prisoners are displayed, along with other penal memorabilia, such as a 'lashing triangle', last used in the enlightened year of 1958. The best-known character on death row, the celebrated bushranger Ned Kelly, was executed here on Melbourne Cup Day 1880. The jail displays the weird suit of improvised armor he was wearing when captured. And you can step inside the executive-sized cell that was his last residence on earth; it has a fine view of the gallows.

Melbourne Museum (open: daily 10am–5pm), the largest ◀ museum complex south of the equator, opened in 2000. It includes Bunjilaka (an Aboriginal centre), the Pasifika Gallery (Pacific artefacts), a Living Forest Gallery, a Science and Life Gallery, a Children's Museum, a theatre and a range of performance spaces. The Australia Gallery houses an equine shrine: the taxidermist's version of Phar Lap – the chestnut gelding considered to be the nation's greatest racehorse, and still a national hero. Phar Lap won the 1930 Melbourne Cup by three lengths, but his heart suddenly failed in 1932, after he won California's Agua Caliente Handicap.

And now for something livelier. Melbourne's **Chinatown** centres on Little Bourke Street, to the east of Swanston Street. Special street lights and gates define the area, in which you'll find Chinese restaurants jammed shoulder to shoulder with cafés, a church, small factories and exotic shops. The area has had a unique flavour since the gold rush days, when fortune-hunters from China crowded into this low-rent district before and after their efforts out in the bush. Chinatown today glows on the maps of local gourmets.

So does **Queen Victoria Market**, which sums up the bounty of Australian agriculture. Just about everything that grows can be found here, piled up in irresistibly fresh pyramids. It's as if the best fruit and vegetables had been borrowed from every market from Sweden to Sicily. The best time to take in the atmosphere is early in the morning, but note that Queen Victoria Market is closed on Mondays and Wednesdays. In addition to produce, you will find a flea market for cheap clothing and bric-a-brac.

Parks and Gardens

South of the river are the **Royal Botanic Gardens** (open: daily Apr–Oct 7.30am–5.30pm; Nov–Mar 7.30am–8.30pm), classed among the finest in the world. Thirty-six hectares (90 acres) of superb rolling landscape remind the visitor that Melbourne has four seasons. Each time of year has its specialities, and seasonal leaflets are available for self-guide walks. For Australians, some of the joy of this park is the selection of brightly tinted trees and plants collected from the Northern Hemisphere. A total of 13,000 species are represented here, in addition to the lovely lawns and lakes.

Between the Botanic Gardens and Kings Domain is the imposing **Government House**, the state governor's mansion, and **La Trobe's Cottage**, its early 19th-century predecessor. The timber cottage was shipped over from Britain to serve as a prefabricated home for Charles La Trobe, who became Victoria's first Lieutenant-Governor back in 1851. One of La Trobe's achievements was to establish a wine industry in Victoria.

Across from the cottage, the massive **Shrine of Remembrance** (open: daily 10am–5pm) commemorates those Australians who fell in World War I; tragically, more than 60 percent of all Australian troops were either killed or wounded in the 'war to end all wars'. Once a year, every Armistice Day at 11am, a beam of sunlight coming through an opening in the roof strikes the Rock of Remembrance. It is a truly powerful and poignant experience.

In Parkville, to the north of the city centre, the **Royal Melbourne Zoological Gardens** (open: daily 9am–5pm)

Melbourne's Royal Botanic Gardens were laid out in the 1850s

charm foreign visitors with kangaroos, koalas, platypuses and other such animals, while amazing the locals with an all-star cast of elephants, giraffes, monkeys and other creatures from far-flung countries. In summer, musical entertainment is provided.

Melbourne's Suburbs

The inner city suburb of **Carlton** combines the restored elegance of Victorian architecture with contemporary dynamism. The latter may be attributed to the area's immigrant colony, mostly Italian. Hence there is a great profusion of outdoor cafés, pizzerias, trattorias and gelaterias.

Lygon Street, Carlton, is Melbourne's slice of Italy, replete with pasta restaurants interspersed with wine bars, cheese shops, quality fashion boutiques and delicatessens. Jimmy Watson's bar and restaurant in Lygon Street is a Melbourne institution.

In **South Yarra**, about 2 hectares (5 acres) of lawns and gardens surround Melbourne's finest stately home, **Como House** (open: daily 10am–5pm). Now run by the National Trust, this example of the colonial era's high style was completed with the addition of a gold-and-white ballroom in the 1870s. Each of its two stories was built with wide verandahs decorated with intricate ironwork.

Toorak, the snootiest of suburbs, is rumoured to harbour more money than any other suburb in Australia. The mansions, nicely landscaped, make tourists and most other passers-by stand and gape. Shopping on Toorak Road is full of stylish delights.

Puffing Billy puffs through the Dandenong Ranges

A totally different shopping experience awaits in the seaside suburb of **St Kilda**. On Sundays its Esplanade is taken over by artists, antiques dealers and flea market entrepreneurs of every sort. Acland Street's restaurants, cafés and bakeries preserve a middle-European Jewish flavour.

Brunswick Street, in **Fitzroy**, reflects the city's bohemian side. Restaurants and cafés, Spanish bars, comedy and live-band venues – all buzzing with activity day and night. Fitzroy's streets are crammed with alternative lifestyle shops, second-hand clothing and funky furniture.

Excursions

A favourite day trip from Melbourne goes out to the **Dandenong Ranges**, volcanic mountains where flowered hillsides and eucalyptus forests set the scene for total relaxation. Only an hour's drive from town, the mountains won't exactly take your breath away; Mt Dandenong itself claims an altitude of only 633m (2,077ft).

One highlight of a day among the small towns, farms, parks and gardens of the Dandenongs is a ride on **Puffing Billy**, a restored old steam train plying 13km (8 miles) of narrow-gauge track. The line was given over to passenger operations from 1900 to 1958. Four years later it was converted to the tourism business. The train never achieves great speed. In fact, an annual race pits Puffing Billy against hundreds of runners.

The **William Ricketts Sanctuary** (open: daily 10am–4.30pm) is an extraordinary collection of sculpture produced by a caucasion loner who was obsessed with Aboriginal culture and its near-destruction by his fellow-whites. Ricketts carved incredibly lifelike faces of Aboriginal people, accompanied by their spiritual symbols. The result of his artistic toils is unorthodox, and may even be found unnerving.

In **Sherbrooke Forest Park** you can give your lungs a treat, savouring the elixir of ferns and mountain ash and whatever flowers happen to be in bloom. The forest is immensely tall, with mountain ash monuments as high as 20-storey buildings and ferns as big as palm trees. This is the place to see – or at least hear – the lyrebird, a great mimic; it does imitations of other birds, human voices and even of inanimate objects such as passing cars. Among the animal residents of the park is the echidna, alias the spiny anteater.

Healesville, less than 60km (37 miles) to the east of Melbourne, is the place to go for an intimate look at Australian animals on their home ground. **Healesville Sanctuary**, nearby

A hot-air balloon drifts over the Yarra Valley wine fields

in the **Yarra Valley** (open: daily 9am–5pm), contains more than 200 native species such as kangaroos, wombats and emus. The animals seem quite comfortable mingling with the visitors, hoping to share a picnic. The sanctuary was founded in 1921 as a research establishment for the study of the local fauna, and is committed to the care of Australian wildlife and the conservation of endangered species.

The Yarra Valley was the site of the first commercial winery in the state, dating back to the middle of the 19th century. The region's vineyards are world-class; well worth a wine-tasting outing.

Phillip Island

For a magical experience for both adults and children, try a long day-trip to **Phillip Island**, home of the fairy penguins (also known as little penguins), the world's smallest members of the penguin family. Hundreds of these engaging birds, standing about 40cm (16in) high and looking quite formal in their blue-grey plumage with white fronts, come home at sunset. The number varies depending on activities at sea, where they spend most of their time fishing.

For reasons of their own, perhaps sensing danger, they tread water offshore until night falls, and only then do they venture onto the beach. After decades of being stared at by visitors, they still feel insecure arriving on the island.

Before dusk falls, hundreds of tourists gather behind ropes on Summerland Beach and in viewing platforms on the sandhills above. You're not allowed to do anything that might upset the penguins: no flash photography, no running, no sudden movement. The penguins observe all this and wait for the first star to appear in the sky.

Then the first brave penguin scout scrambles onto dry land and suspiciously lurches across the beach and up the hill to his burrow. In small groups the others follow, waddling through the sand dunes up to their burrows right at sunset, just as their ancestors have done night after night for thousands of generations. It can take half an hour or more for all the birds that are coming ashore to arrive.

Phillip Island, which is situated 120km (75 miles) southeast of Melbourne, has about 2 million visitors a year. The visitor centre here has a simulated underwater display where you can study the penguins' life at sea. The island is linked to the mainland by a bridge at San Remo.

The penguins are the stars, but the supporting cast is also well worth seeing: thousands of fur seals residing on tall rocks on the west coast (early December, the peak of the breeding season, is the best time to see them); clouds of mutton birds arriving each November from their wintering grounds thousands of miles away; and a colony of koalas, vegetating in the high branches of the gum trees. Take a sweater or coat for the penguin parade, for the nights are chilly even in summer.

Wilsons Promontory

Until the Ice Age, the southernmost tip of the Australian mainland was connected to Tasmania. When the ice melted the heights became an island. Since then the dunes have built up, linking the massive promontory to the rest of Victoria. The varied and spectacular scenery has made **Wilsons Promontory** the state's most popular national park.

The coastline ranges from magnificent granite headlands to peaceful sandy beaches. Walking trails wander through forests and moorland and flower-covered heathland. Koalas live here, as do kangaroos and emus. Known locally as 'The Prom', the peninsula is about 240km (150 miles) southeast of Melbourne.

About an hour's drive west of Wilsons Promontory, on Bass Highway, the **Giant Earthworm Museum** displays a bizarre life-form that you probably won't encounter anywhere else. *Megasolides australis* is a giant gurgling earthworm native to this region. It's the world's largest terrestrial invertebrate. The worm's gurgling (the sound of its passage through the ground) is sufficiently loud to interrupt human conversation on the surface. It's enough to ruin your lunch. The museum (part of a nature theme park called Wildlife Wonderland, open daily 10am–5pm) explains the life-cycle of the worm. An average specimen grows to about 3m (almost 10ft) long, and some grow to about 5m (16ft).

An interactive display in the earthworm museum allows you to walk through a mock-up of the worm's stomach and listen to the sound of its heartbeat and the flowing of its blood. You can also see the worms themselves.

The Goldfields

A drive of 113km (70 miles) west of Melbourne takes you well over a century back in time to the attractive town of **Ballarat**, rich with all the atmosphere of Australia's golden age. This is real gold-rush country, and it is still a prize destination for tourists.

Ballarat has a bittersweet history. Gold was discovered in 1851, and thousands of miners trekked to the fields. The early arrivals simply scooped up a fortune, but latecomers had to work harder, following the ore ever deeper.

Almost from the outset the government collected a licence fee from the miners. Many newcomers couldn't afford to pay a tax, so they tended to lie low when the licence inspectors swooped. In the midst of growing antagonism between the

Panning for gold at Ballarat

authorities and the miners, charges of murder and official corruption pushed the diggers to revolt. In the Eureka Rebellion, Australia's first and only uprising, insurgent miners were besieged in their stockade. An uneven battle cost many people their lives, mostly diggers. The nation was stunned. The anguish endured for years, inspiring poets and politicians.

When peace returned to the goldfields, and many of the miners' grievances were answered, Ballarat went back to the business of making a fortune. In 1858 a group of Cornishmen came upon what they called the Welcome Nugget, which weighed in at an enormous 63,000g (2,220oz). It was eventually put on show in the Crystal Palace in London before being minted. Parallel with the discovery of wealth,

Ballarat grew into a stately town where even art and good taste had their day.

To see what Ballarat was like in the 1850s, visit **Sovereign Hill** (open: daily 10am–5pm), an open-air museum re-creating the sights, sounds and smells of the gold rush. Local folk dressed in Victorian-era clothing operate the old shops, post office, bakery and printing office of what appears to be a real town. Tourists are invited to try their hand with a digger's pan, under expert instruction. The **Gold Museum** (open: daily 9.30am–5.30pm) traces the history of the mineral since biblical times and displays notable nuggets and gold coins.

In the real Ballarat, the principal public buildings on the town's wide tree-lined streets are a long-lasting monument to the good old days. Some of those who got rich quick had the good taste to spend some of their money on the finer things. Hence the statues of mythological subjects in marble

Main Street, Sovereign Hill, re-creating Ballarat in the 1850s

in the **Botanical Gardens**, and the admirable collection of early Australian art in the **Ballarat Fine Arts Gallery** (open: daily 10.30am–5pm).

Another treat for nostalgia fans is the town of **Bendigo**, situated 150km (93 miles) northwest of Melbourne. The town's unusual name is a very roundabout corruption of Abednego, the Old Testament companion of Shadrach and Meshach. In the 1850s, Bendigo Creek, running through the centre of town, was besieged with panning miners.

The **Central Deborah Mine** (open: daily 9.30am–5pm) is now a museum of 19th-century mining technology. From there you can take a 'Talking Tram', an antique vehicle rigged up for tourists on an 8-km (5-mile) historic itinerary. The last stop is the **joss house**. One curiosity of Bendigo was the size of the Chinese population. Chinese miners, who enjoyed less than harmony with their white neighbours, worshipped in a prayer house constructed of timber and handmade bricks. The remains that stand today are filled with relics of the early Chinese fortune hunters.

The Great Ocean Road

Beyond Torquay is the beginning of the Great Ocean Road, which skirts nearly 200km (125 miles) of spectacular coast-line and is undoubtedly one of the world's most beautiful drives. It was built by ex-serviceman of the World War I in homage to their comrades killed at the front.

A great number of ships have gone aground in these treacherous waters. Along **Shipwreck Coast**, the wrecks of more than 80 sailing vessels rest on the seabed. But the surf provides recreation, too: **Bells Beach**, situated between Torquay and Anglesea, hosts the Bells Surfing Classic every Easter. Just before you reach Lorne, follow the signs for **Erskine Falls**, splendid cascades which are worth the 20-minute detour. **Lorne**, on the edge of beautiful **Apollo Bay**,

London Bridge, one of the sights of the Great Ocean Road

is a popular seaside resort, well provided with restaurants, cafés and shops.

From Apollo Bay, the Great Ocean Road leaves the coast to wind through the forest behind **Cape Otway**, where the lighthouse has watched over the entrance to the Bass Strait since 1848. **Otway National Park**, not far from the coast, offers the chance to see swamp wallabies and possibly koalas, echidnas and emus.

Beyond Princetown lies the spectacular coastline of **Port Campbell National Park**, where breakers have battered the soft limestone cliffs, creating grottoes and gorges, arches and sea-sculptures rising from the surf. The Great Ocean Road allows only occasional glimpses of the drama below, which includes the stark rock stacks known as the **Twelve Apostles** and the spray billowing through the arch of **London Bridge**. Take the time to stop at all the vantage points: they overlook Victoria's most dramatic array of sights.

After Peterborough and the spectacular Bay of Islands comes **Warrnambool**, once a busy port and now a pastoral and holiday centre. Around the original lighthouse is the **Flagstaff Hill Maritime Museum** (open: daily 9am–5pm), a recreation of a 19th-century port with its shipwrights, chandlers and sailmakers.

Along the coast is the fishing-village charm of **Port Fairy**, where brightly-painted boats tie up at the jetty with their catches of lobster and crab. Traditionally the birthplace of Victoria, Port Fairy was named by Captain James Wishart who brought his tiny cutter, the *Fairy*, into the Moyne River to find shelter during a sealing expedition in 1810. Sealers and, later, whalers built quaint stone cottages which still nestle under the tall Norfolk Island pines shading the streets.

TASMANIA

If you thought of Tasmania as the last stop before the South Pole, you're right: Antarctic expeditions actually set sail from Hobart. No matter what direction you're heading in, it's a staging post you will hate to leave. Tasmania's scenery owes more to solar than polar influences. Although snow covers the hills in winter, it's a verdant island enjoying a temperate climate. Summer even brings shirtsleeve weather, and you can find palm trees as well as poplars and oaks for some shade.

Suspended 240km (149 miles) to the south of southernmost mainland Australia, Tasmania is small only by the swollen standards of the continent. With an area of approximately 68,000 sq km (26,250 sq miles), it's bigger than Sri Lanka or Switzerland.

'Tassie', as the state is familiarly known, calls itself the Holiday Isle and pushes tourism. Its early residents would have had a bitter laugh at that, interspersed with an oath or two, for the island used to be the place where the really incorrigible prisoners were sent. While humble embezzlers and petty larcenists were transported to Sydney, the batterers and escape artists tended to be tagged for Tasmania.

Early explorers happened upon Tasmania because it lies on the 40th parallel – the Roaring Forties, along which an unfailing westerly wind blows around the globe. Their sailing ships could hardly miss the place. But that's not to diminish the achievement of the Dutch navigator Abel Tasman, who gets credit for discovering the island in 1642. He named it after his sponsor, Anton van Diemen, governor of the Dutch East Indies.

The Dutch never saw a future for Van Diemen's Land, and Britain eventually claimed the island simply to cut out the French. Because of the cruel conditions inflicted on the British prisoners, Van Diemen's Land acquired a sinister

Wiping out the Aborigines

When Van Diemen's Land was first settled, the island's Aboriginal people numbered between 3,000 and 7,000. They were different from the indigenous mainland peoples, in looks and culture. As the British seized the land and wiped out the animals and birds that the indigenous tribes needed for food, the Aborigines fought back with punitive attacks. Enraged, the white men retaliated with all the force at their disposal. The survivors of this pogrom were exiled to Flinders Island, an outpost best known for its shipwrecks. There they joined a handful of Aboriginal women who had been abducted by British and American whalers and sealers and taken to the island to serve as concubines or slaves. Although there were belated efforts to protect the race, the last of the full-blooded Tasmanian tribesmen died in 1876. The race was not entirely exterminated, however, as mixed-blood descendants of some of the Flinders Island exiles have since moved to Tasmania and founded a flourishing Aboriginal movement there.

reputation. The very mention of the name could send a shiver down a sinner's spine. The transportation of convicts was abolished in 1852, and some three years later the name was changed to Tasmania in memory of its discoverer and to improve the state's image.

The lush pastures of Tasmania

Since then, Tasmania has become something of a tourist paradise. One day, some brilliant entrepreneur may put it on the world map and the crowds will arrive. Until then, if you like wild scenery, open moors, rolling green hills, deserted beaches, Georgian architecture, temperate-climate forests, uncrowded towns and open-hearted people, you could easily become a Tasmaniac.

Hobart

Everybody knows that Sydney Harbour is the exciting one, glamorous and instantly recognisable all over the world. Hobart is the lovable harbour, a perfect ocean port on a dreamy river, with soft mountains rising beyond. It might have been transplanted from quite another seafaring latitude, as brisk and tidy as Bergen or Helsinki.

You never know what kind of ships you'll see here: freighters from Singapore, floating fish factories from Japan, or yachts from distant islands – perhaps Britain or Bermuda. The arrival of an ancient sealer, whaler or windjammer in the harbour would be right in character. Sail power still matters here: Hobart's Constitution Dock is the finishing line of the gruelling Sydney-to-Hobart yacht race.

Hobart, Australia's second oldest capital city, has kept a powerful array of historic monuments, from stately official buildings to quaint cottages. Best of all, they're spick and span and still in use.

With a population of around 194,000 (suburbs included), Hobart is small enough to get around and get to know, and as unsophisticated and satisfying as the local fish and chips.

In this deepwater port, the ships come right into the centre of town. The waterfront, always colourful, is the place to begin exploring the city on foot. You can watch crates of giant crabs and scallops coming ashore, and follow their destiny to the floating fast-food restaurants moored here. Just behind **Constitution Dock**, where the yacht races end, the late Victorian-era **Customs House** stands out as one of the city's most imposing sandstone monuments. It was built at the beginning of the 20th century on the site of one of the colony's oldest landmarks, the original customs house.

Also bordering the docks, **Salamanca Place** is home to a long row of sandstone warehouses from the 1830s, restored and proudly occupied by artisans' workshops, boutiques and restaurants. On Saturday mornings, stalls selling various arts and crafts, knick-knacks, flowers and vegetables cover the cobblestones; jugglers, mimes and minstrels perform and pass the hat.

Altogether more serious is **Parliament House**, also facing the waterfront, built in 1840. The state's bicameral legislature operates in a low-rise stone building which displays some admirable architectural details.

Another venerable structure still in use is the **Theatre Royal** on Campbell Street, Australia's oldest live theatre. Built in the most exquisitely luxurious style in 1834, it has featured stars like Noel Coward and Laurence Olivier.

Overlooking Salamanca Place, **Battery Point** is the historic heart of Hobart, beautifully preserved. The battery in question was a set of coastal artillery guns installed in 1818. Ten years later signal flags were added, for relaying the big news of the day, such as ship arrivals or prison escapes. The area is worth an hour or two of exploration on foot, to absorb the atmosphere of the narrow streets, the mansions and cottages, churches and taverns.

Racing from Sydney to Hobart

One of the upper-class colonial homes has been turned into the **Van Diemen's Land Memorial Folk Museum** (open: Tues–Fri 10am–5pm, Sat–Sun 2–5pm), which is devoted to the colony's 19th-century way of life, and displays artefacts from toys to farm equipment.

The **Tasmanian Museum and Art Gallery** (open: daily 10am–5pm) is worth visiting for its collection relating to the Tasmanian tiger (thylacine). This handsome, striped, dog-like marsupial is believed to have been hunted to extinction by the 1930s, although some people swear they have sighted living specimens in remote regions.

The centre of Hobart is linked to the suburbs and the airport by the graceful **Tasman Bridge** across the Derwent River. The pre-stressed concrete bridge ran into trouble in 1975; more accurately, trouble ran into the bridge. A bulk ore carrier, off course, ploughed into the span of the bridge; tragically, four cars tumbled into the river and the ship sank.

Hobart harbour, one of the loveliest in the world

For an expansive panorama of Hobart and the valley of the Derwent, ascend **Mt Wellington**, the city's most prominent landmark. It is named in appreciation of the Duke of Wellington. For this expedition you can forget your mountain-climbing equipment. A paved road goes all the way to the summit, 1,270m (4,167ft) above the sea. It often snows on the mountain in the winter months – an exciting novelty for tourists from more northerly Australian climes – but it rarely blocks the road.

Excursions from Hobart

A popular tourist destination up the river at Claremont is the **Cadbury chocolate factory** (guided tours Mon–Fri). Fans of Willy Wonka just love it – and guided tours include as much chocolate as you can eat. The tours attract sweet-toothed visitors of all ages, but tots under eight must be carried.

Those with a more savoury tooth might prefer touring the imposing **Cascade Brewery**, the oldest in Australia, at 140 Cascade Road. The beer, made with pure Tasmanian water, is excellent. Cascade uses a Tasmanian tiger logo in its advertising and on its labels.

At **Taroona**, situated beyond Wrest Point, you can visit the remains, more than a century old, of a different kind of factory, the **Shot Tower**. Though it looks like an ordinary chimney, this tower 60m (197ft) tall, was used in the manufacture of gunshot and musket balls. Molten lead was dropped from the top of the tower into cold water, and solidified in a perfectly spherical shape. You can climb the internal spiral staircase to the very summit for a view of the countryside.

A complex of modern office buildings at **Kingston** is the working headquarters for Australia's extensive operations in the neighbourhood of the South Pole. The Commonwealth Antarctic Division coordinates logistics and research in fields such as glaciology, botany, physics and medicine. Inside the main building are displays of sleds and faded flags from the early pioneering expeditions.

Launceston

Tasmania's second city is an agreeable, roomy town at the head of the Tamar River. Launceston exudes an unexpected English flavour, with elm trees, rosebushes, and patriotic statues and plaques. The journey north from Hobart skirts soft green hills studded with sheep. In the villages, to enliven the scene, the houses have roofs the colour of fire engines.

Launceston was founded in the year 1805 as Patersonia. Soon afterwards, the name was changed to that of the town of Launceston in Cornwall, the birthplace of

> **The wineries around Launceston offer tastings, and most of them also have very good restaurants.**

the colony's governor. The historic aspects of the town are well preserved, starting in the centre, the **City Square**. Here, grouped together, are a modern pyramid-style state office building, a Japanese garden and a building from 1830, **Macquarie House**. Restored to mint condition, this sometime warehouse, barracks and office building now serves as part of the local museum (open: Mon–Sat 10am–4pm).

The main building of the **Queen Victoria Museum** (open: daily 10am–5pm), situated just a short stroll away on Wellington Street, has something for everyone, from stuffed platypuses to blunderbusses, from prisoners' chains to an invigorating collection of modern art. One surprising attraction here is an intact joss house which originally served the Chinese tin miners in the Tasmanian town of Weldborough. Downstairs, the Queen Vic Café is one of Launceston's best.

Life in early 19th-century Tasmania is recaptured at **Penny Royal World**. Here, a corn mill built in 1825 has been reconstituted, and a cannon foundry and arsenal created to demonstrate the stages of gunpowder manufacture, from the distillation of saltpetre to the finished cannonballs. Another attraction is the paddle-steamer *Lady Stelfox*. You can take a 45-minute ride on it.

Just around the bend is the **Cataract Gorge**, a stirring geological feature within walking distance of the centre of town. Here the South Esk River slices between steep cliffs on its way to the Tamar. There are hiking trails, boating opportunities and, for sightseers who don't suffer queasy spells, a chairlift – the longest single-span lift in the world at 282m (924ft) – spans the canyon from on high.

Port Arthur

Tasmania's most-visited historic highlight is the old penal colony of **Port Arthur**, an hour's drive from Hobart. Port Arthur's past is so grim, you'll be astonished at just how picturesque it looks. Founded in 1830 as Australia's ultimate prison settlement, Port Arthur housed the most troublesome and intractable convicts – those who had committed second offences after being transported to Australia. It rapidly became one of the world's most-dreaded institutions, reputedly even more brutal than the French penal colony of Devil's Island in South America.

Chain gangs, toiling under the lash, built the solid stone buildings, which you see here today and have survived more than a century of abandonment, fire, storm and looting.

The biggest building still standing, at four storeys high, was designed originally as a storehouse but became a penitentiary for 650 inmates. Other surviving buildings are the **Lunatic Asylum** (many prisoners went mad) and, next door, the 'model' prison. Both have been restored. Convicts designed and built a large church, now in ruins. Its 13 spires represent

Port Arthur: an attractive town with a grim history

Christ and the apostles. Then there is the mortuary, which did a lively business; more than 1,700 graves occupy the nearby **Isle of the Dead**. Other than by dying, Port Arthur was practically escape-proof, with sharks waiting on one side and half-starved killer dogs on the other. In total, some 10,000 prisoners did time at Port Arthur during its 47 years of operation.

As if that legacy of suffering wasn't enough, Port Arthur hit the headlines for the wrong reasons in 1996, when a maniacal visitor gunned down 53 men, women and children, killing 35, in the world's worst peacetime massacre.

Wilderness

For many Australians from the other side of the Bass Strait, Tasmania is the closest they can get to European-style scenery. At such a distance from Europe, though, the landscape is almost untouched by civilisation. There is one good reason why it has remained unspoiled: it's often unapproachable by road. Four-wheel-drive vehicles, canoes, rafts or just sturdy legs are the best methods of penetrating these wild places. In Tasmania a higher percentage of the total area has been set aside as national parks than in any other state.

Even so, attempts by various commercial interests to log or dam unspoiled wilderness regions have triggered notable clashes with Tasmania's strong conservationist movement. According to the Wilderness Society of Tasmania, over 22,000 hectares (54,361 acres) of native forest were logged in the state in 1999, nearly two-thirds in pure, 'old-growth' forest. In every Australian state other than Tasmania, the logging of pure rainforest has been banned. Fortunately, much Tasmanian forest remains, national parks proliferate and the interests of conservation and responsible tourism – as opposed to those of the logging and wood-chipping industries – may yet prevail.

South West National Park covers nearly all of the southwestern corner of Tasmania, and contains a variety of spectacular scenery, including rugged mountains, glacial lakes, icy rivers and forests of giant Antarctic beeches. One recent feature of the region is the new **Lake Pedder**, flooded to 25 times its natural size for a hydroelectric scheme. For better or worse, the controversial project brought the first roads to the area.

A few hours' drive northwest of Hobart is **Cradle Mountain–Lake St Clair National Park**. Here you'll discover a savage wonder-

The grandeur of Cradle Mountain

land, filled by mountain peaks and waterfalls, temperate rainforests and clear lakes astir with trout. The wildlife is all around you: wallabies, possums, Tasmanian devils and wildcats. If the Tasmanian tiger wasn't thought to be extinct, this would probably be the place to find one.

Mt Field National Park, just an hour's drive from Hobart, is popular in the winter as an easy-to-reach, no-fuss skiing area. In the summer months the heathlands beyond the giant forests burst into bloom, creating a carpet of alpine flowers, although some areas are covered with pesky thickets of horizontal scrub, a Tasmanian speciality. At the entrance to the national park is a village with the engaging name of National Park.

WHAT TO DO

SPORT

Sporting life in Australia is inescapable, from the dawn jogger puffing past your window to the football crowds celebrating late into the night with shouting, songs and car horns. In a country so beautiful, and with a climate so benign, you'll be tempted to join the sporting crowds, either playing the game yourself or watching the professionals. Under the dependable sun, everything is possible, from skiing – on water or snow – to surfing to sailing.

Sports, it's often said, are a passion Down Under. You can measure their impact by the newspapers, with their comprehensive sports sections, and by the amount of live sports coverage and results on television and radio. If Australians are not playing a game or watching it, they're most likely betting on the result, or at least arguing about it.

In what other country could a racehorse be as revered as is Phar Lap, winner of the 1930 Melbourne Cup? When he died, after a heroic victory in the United States, flags flew at half-mast in Sydney. Today Phar Lap's body is the star attraction in Melbourne Museum's Australia Gallery, and his mighty heart is preserved at the National Museum in Canberra. The Melbourne Cup race itself brings the nation to a temporary halt as everyone tunes in to listen.

But sporting tastes have changed over time. More than a century ago, a guidebook gloomily reported that very little hunting was available around Sydney, except when 'occasionally parties are made up for rabbit, wallaby or kangaroo shooting'. In 1903 the first car race was run in Australia. Three years later, daringly, surf bathing in the daytime became legal in Sydney. And waterskiing caught on in 1936. Australia won the Davis Cup in 1939. When Melbourne hosted the Olympic Games in 1956, Aussie athletes seized 35 of the medals. The world was becoming aware of Australia as one of the foremost sporting powers, a nation of hardy, aggressive competitors who could become champions in fields as varied as tennis and swimming, cricket and golf, athletics and rugby.

In 1983, joyous delirium swept the nation when the yacht *Australia II* captured the America's Cup. At the 1996 Atlanta Olympics, Australia was more successful per head of population than any of the top 20 countries. In 2000, at the Sydney Olympics, Australia came fourth in the medal tally (after the US, Russia and China). Australia very nearly came third – it collected 58 medals, against China's 59. Australia's Olympic achievement in out-performing countries like Germany, France, Britain and Japan is even more remarkable considering its population – just 19 million.

A racing crew launch their boat at Leighton Beach, Perth

Watersports

Australia's endless coastline provides enough beaches, coves and ports to keep the nation in the swim all year round. If that isn't enough, there are lakes, rivers and swimming pools, both Olympic-size and backyard versions. Watersports of every variety are here for the taking.

Swimming in the Indian Ocean, the Tasman Sea, or the Coral Sea is the sort of sport you'll long remember. But the surf can be as dangerous as it is invigorating. Most of the popular beaches are delineated by flags showing where it's safe to swim. Beware of undertow or shifting currents and always obey the instructions of lifeguards. Sharks are a problem in some areas, with occasional attacks on bathers, and very occasional fatalities. When a shark alert is sounded, beat an immediate retreat to the shore and ask questions later.

Diving amid the colourful fauna of the Great Barrier Reef

In spite of their mild-sounding name, box jelly-fish are a serious seasonal danger, especially in the north; elsewhere there may be Portuguese men-of-war, sea snakes or other silent menaces. Check locally before you even put a foot in the surf.

A final word of caution: before you stretch out on the beach, make sure that you protect yourself from the sun, which is more powerful than you think. Light complexions are particularly vulnerable to quick, painful sunburn and worse.

Snorkelling brings you into intimate contact with a brilliant new world full of multicoloured fish and coral. The sport requires a minimum of equipment – a mask

> The world's first life-saving club was set up at Bondi Beach in 1906. The first surfers took to the water (also at Bondi) in 1912.

and breathing tube and, optionally, flippers to expand your range of operations. Practically anyone can learn how to snorkel in a matter of minutes, and there is no great skill or stamina required.

Scuba diving with an air tank is the advanced version of snorkeling. The best place in Australia for scuba outings – and quite possibly the best place in the world – is the coral wonderland of the Great Barrier Reef. Some of the resort islands are equipped for all the needs of divers, though you may have to supply your own regulator and demand valves. If you want to learn the sport, some resorts have weekly courses starting in the swimming pool or a quiet cove, and leading up to an Open Water Certificate. Elsewhere along Australia's coasts, some serious scuba divers devote themselves to exploring submerged wrecks.

Surfing: Yet another discovery by the intrepid Captain Cook, who came upon this sport in Hawaii. He wrote: 'The boldness and address with which we saw them perform these difficult and dangerous manoeuvres was altogether astonishing...' It was nearly two centuries before the first world championships were to be held in Sydney. Surfing areas are marked by signs, flags or discs. The best-known surfing zone in the country must be Sydney's Bondi Beach, but there are many other fine locations up and down the coast of New South Wales. Although Queensland's Surfers Paradise may

Surfing, a popular Australian pastime, was introduced from Hawaii

be just that, many of the experts prefer the giant rollers far-ther north at Noosa. Victoria's most popular surfing area is around Torquay. On the west coast, there are easily accessi-ble surfing beaches near Perth and Bunbury.

Sailing: Visiting yachts and their crews will always get a warm Aussie-style welcome. At popular resorts, for instance along the Gold Coast or the Great Barrier Reef, yachts and powerboats can be chartered, with or without a professional skipper. Inland, you can command a sailing boat or a house-boat on the relaxing Murray River. Or you might just want to settle for an hour's rental of a pedal boat.

Fishing: You'll need a licence to fish inland waters in some states, but the sea is free for all amateurs. Outstanding trout fishing is found in Tasmania and the Snowy Mountains. Seasons and bag limits vary with the district. As for game fishing, the challenge of the giant black marlin is best met off the northern coast of Queensland. If your catch weighs less than half a ton, it's polite to throw the little fellow back. Or settle for tuna, mackerel or sailfish. Good deep-sea fishing is also found off the coast of Western Australia, especially at Geraldton, and in the Spencer Gulf, near Adelaide. In the north, a coveted game fish is the barramundi – a great fighter prized for its delicate flesh.

Sports Ashore

Golf: The landscaping may be foreign, the climate may be a better year-round bet than you're accustomed to, but the game's the same. Melbourne considers itself the nation's golfing capital, with championship courses such as Victoria and the Royal Melbourne. All the cities have golf clubs; they often operate under exchange agreements with clubs overseas, or you may have to be introduced by a local member. With no formality at all you can rent a set of clubs and play at one of the public courses to be found in all the sizeable towns. Golf is also a popular spectator sport in Australia. The Australian Open takes place in November.

Tennis: Having produced so many illustrious tennis champions, Australia takes the game seriously. You'll find courts available in the towns and resorts; some rent rackets and shoes. If you're just watching, then join the crowd. The biggest throng ever to watch a Davis Cup match was counted in Sydney in 1954: more than 25,000 fans. The world's top tennis stars usually tour Australia in December and January. Melbourne Park (formerly Flinders Park) hosts the Australian Open, one of tennis's four Grand Slam tournaments, every January.

Bowling (lawn bowls): All over Australia this leisurely sport finds men and women in cream-coloured costumes, spending hours in the sun decorously bowling on the neatly trimmed grass. If you're a bowler you'll be able to find a game at almost any club.

Skiing: Although Australia does not claim to have invented skiing, fur trappers in Tasmania were getting around on something similar to skis in the 1830s. The season in the Australian Alps usually lasts from June to September, and sometimes into November, which should be inducement enough for skiers from the Northern Hemisphere. The best-known and best-equipped of the ski resorts in the Snowy Mountains include Thredbo Village, Perisher Valley and Smiggin Holes (NSW) and Mt Buller, Falls Creek, Mt Hotham and Mt Buffalo (Victoria).

Football and Rugby

In Australia the subject of football is so vast and complex – for a start, four different kinds of football are played – that the stranger is likely to be left gasping on the sidelines. But since the country is crazy about it, at least a few definitions may be useful. Incidentally, whatever type of football is being discussed, the fans are likely to call it 'footy'.

Australian Rules Football was introduced in Melbourne in 1858, and although the Australian Football League (AFL) now includes teams in most major cities, 'Aussie Rules' finds its most fanatical following in and around Melbourne. It is estimated that, every winter Saturday in the city, one person in 16 attends an AFL game, and thousands more follow the saturation TV coverage. The Grand Final, held at the Melbourne Cricket Ground in September, is one of the great sporting experiences, rivalling an English FA Cup Final or an American Super Bowl for colour, passion and atmosphere.

The sport, which combines elements of rugby, Gaelic football and other

> 'Aussie Rules' was first played by Victoria gold miners in the 1850s, and the Melbourne Football Club was founded in 1858 – but the game's official rules were not established until 1866.

The Aussie Rules grand final in Melbourne attracts huge crowds

forms of the game, is characterised by long-distance kicks and passes and high scoring on an oversized but crowded field – with 18 players to a side.

Rugby League started as a 13-man professional alternative to Rugby Union, and is played today mainly in Sydney, Brisbane and Canberra. It's a roughhouse game, physical rather than cerebral, based on an uncompromising masochistic style of defence that prompted one American football coach to observe: 'Our guys could never stand up to that sort of constant punishment.' League attendances are nothing like as large as those of the AFL, but the Sydney clubs – such as St George, Western Suburbs, Many and Paramatta – keep their star players fabulously well paid through the revenue from their slot machines and licensed clubs. The Aussie national side, known as the Kangaroos, regularly hops through tours of France and Great Britain unbeaten.

Rugby Union, the 15-a-side, formerly amateur version of the game, is fast, rough and engrossing to the fans. Compared with League, the game traditionally had a 'silvertail' (upper-crust) image based partly on its strength in the universities and private schools. Now that Union is fully and openly professional, the gentlemanly spirit is less in evidence. Since 1995, teams representing New South Wales, Queenland and Australian Capital Territory have competed every winter in the Super 12 tournament, against sides from New Zealand and South Africa. The Australian national team, the Wallabies, regularly takes on its two Southern Hemisphere rivals in the Tri-Nations competition.

Soccer is the oldest of the country's games but, compared with the three other species of football, is the poor relation. It

---

Australian Champions

Australia has bred many world-class winners. Below are some of the pre-eminent sporting personalities of the 20th century:

Athletics
- Herb Elliott
- Ron Clarke
- Robert DeCastella
- Cathy Freeman

Motor racing
- Jack Brabham
- Alan Jones
- Peter Brock

Cricket
- Don Bradman
- Greg Chappell
- Dennis Lillee

- Steve Waugh
- Shane Warne

Golf
- Peter Thompson
- Greg Norman
- Stuart Appleby
- Ian Baker-Finch
- Wayne Grady

Swimming
- Dawn Fraser
- Samantha Riley
- Kieren Perkins
- Grant Hackett

- Ian Thorpe
- Michael Klim
- Susan O'Neill

Tennis
- Evonne Goolagong
- Margaret Court
- Rod Laver
- Pat Cash
- Pat Rafter
- Leyton Hewitt
- The 'Woodies'
(Mark Woodforde, Todd Woodbridge)

kicked off in the 19th century among earnest British migrants, more or less stagnated until after World War II, then was revitalised by the arrival of immigrants from southern Europe. Today most clubs in the National Soccer League are dominated by players from the Italian, Greek, Croatian, Slavic, Maltese, Dutch and Macedonian communities.

Most towns have a racecourse: this is Townsville, Queensland

Other Spectator Sports

The Australians have been playing **cricket** since the early days of the penal colony at Sydney Cove. In its traditional form, the game can go on for five days, and even then it may finish in a draw. It was the Aussie media mogul Kerry Packer who had the temerity to make a show-biz spectacle out of a gentlemanly pursuit, staging games at night under floodlights, in gaudy uniforms, and ending the match decisively in a single day. Fortunately for conservative fans, the old-fashioned Test survives as well under the Australian sun, and the current Aussie team is recognised as the strongest in the world at the five-day game. The season extends from October to the end of March, with matches played at interstate level (the Sheffield Shield), down through district ranks to the junior and social levels.

Horseracing: Practically every Australian town, even in the Outback, has a racecourse, and the big cities tend to have more than one. The best times to go to the races are Saturdays and holidays. Betting on horses, or most other things, is as Australian as ice-cold beer. Enthusiasts who can't make it to the course can participate in their own way through off-track betting facilities, legal and computerised and called TAB for Totalisator Agency Board. For punters who prefer to patronise illegal bookmakers, they are seldom far away.

The biggest competition of the year in the Australian horse-racing season is the Melbourne Cup, a two-mile classic that is followed so obsessively that the day it is run – the first Tuesday in November – is a legal holiday in Victoria. Even the process of government is suspended so that the nation's decision-makers in Canberra can watch the live telecast.

Every September in the remote Outback town of Birdsville in Queensland, the Birdsville Picnic Races attract enormous crowds. The population of Birdsville leaps from 30 to 3,000 overnight, with many spectators arriving by light planes from all over Australia.

Trotting (harness racing) can be seen in big cities and some provincial locations. In the capital cities the trotters run at night under floodlights.

Greyhound racing is another spectacle that draws crowds of punters. The dogs usually run in the cool of the evening; the audiences at the track can be as fascinating as the sport itself.

Motor racing: Big races take place near Brisbane, Sydney and Melbourne. The biggest of all is the Australian Formula 1 Grand Prix in Melbourne, where you can watch the world championship contenders compete.

ENTERTAINMENT

Australia receives the best the world can offer in the performing arts, as well as producing masterpieces of its own. Open any major city newspaper for advertised performances of chamber music, opera, avant-garde plays, Aboriginal theatre, comedy, cabaret, Shakespearean classics, rock concerts, Broadway hits, dance, art shows and touring exhibitions from the top galleries of Europe and North America.

Australia's two largest cities, Sydney and Melbourne, present the greatest number of cultural events, although Adelaide, in South Australia, hosts one of the most extensive and exciting – the Adelaide Festival, held biennially in even-numbered years.

Throughout the country, a lot of racy entertainment can be seen, as well as higher-brow cultural attractions such as opera, ballet, concerts and drama. Between the extremes there's something for everybody who just wants a relaxing evening out.

In some smaller towns, odd events such as cane-toad racing, thong throwing (an open-toed sandal is hurled as far as possible) and brick-throwing draw the crowds. In coastal towns and cities, summer surf carnivals are another favourite – a chance for lifeguards to show off their skills, as well as a celebration of Australian beach culture.

On Stage

Theatre has been going strong in Australia for a couple of centuries. In 1789, scarcely a year after New South Wales was founded, a troupe of convicts put on a Restoration comedy *(The Recruiting Officer)* by George Farquhar as part of the celebrations for the birthday of King George III. The first real theatre opened in Sydney in 1796. Drama

Sydney Opera House also stages ballet, concerts and theatre

The annual Jazz Carnival brings swing to Manly, Sydney

today is at its liveliest in Sydney and Melbourne – mainly because their size ensures a reasonable audience – but you can enjoy performances in most cities.

Opera has attracted keen audiences Down Under since the days of Dame Nellie Melba. In more recent times, the coloratura brilliance of Dame Joan Sutherland spread her fame around the world. Seeing grand opera in the Sydney Opera House makes a gala occasion even more so; but opera-goers in other cities may enjoy better acoustics and atmosphere in their newer theatres.

Ballet and dance: The country's leading classical dance company, the Australian Ballet, founded in 1962, is based in Melbourne but performs in Sydney as well. Leading modern dance troupes include the Sydney Dance Company, the Australian Dance Theatre and the Bangarra Dance Theatre. All varieties of dance have a following, from ballroom dancing (as seen in the Australian movie *Strictly Ballroom*) to tap-dancing (as depicted in the Australian movie *Bootmen*).

Music

Every state and territory in Australia has its own symphony orchestra; many maintain youth and chamber orchestras as well. An influential promoter of serious music, Musica Viva Australia, presents thousands of concerts each year across the country. Sydney holds free – and hugely popular – open-air opera and classical concerts each year in the Domain as part of the Sydney Festival.

Jazz clubs exist in all the big cities, where you might hear a visiting celebrity or an up-and-coming local band. Plenty of pubs feature jazz, but usually at weekends only. Both indoor and outdoor jazz concerts are also advertised.

Other music – folk, pop, rock or rap – can reveal something of a nation's soul. Aussie options range from a bearded troubadour dishing out bush ballads in an Outback saloon to hard-hitting metal bands. Contemporary groups such as Silverchair, Powderfinger and Savage Garden follow in the wake of past notables like the Seekers, the Bee Gees, Men at Work, INXS, Midnight Oil, AC/DC and Cold Chisel.

Nightlife

The scale and sophistication of an evening's entertainment depends on the size of the town. You won't find Jennifer Lopez or Sir Elton John performing in Burrumbuttock, New South Wales, but nightlife in Australia's smaller towns and remoter areas can still be a load of fun, as anyone who has attended an Outback bush dance or seen that wacky Australian movie *The Adventures of Priscilla, Queen of the Desert* will know.

In larger centres and cities, nightlife venues, acts and attractions are listed in guides published in daily newspapers, usually on Thursdays or Fridays. Posters slapped on walls and telegraph poles proclaim dance parties, gigs, plays and concerts. Musical pubs and private clubs provide more mainstream entertainment; it's usually quite easy for non-members to enter the latter.

Clubs subsidise their meals and entertainment with profits from their slot machines, called poker machines (more affectionately, pokies). For punters who prefer to wager serious money, gambling **casinos** are available in big cities and resorts. Usually open very late into the night, casinos are typically equipped for, among other pursuits: roulette, craps, keno, blackjack, baccarat and the backwoods game of two-up *(see page 141)* in a more refined, electronic version.

Cinema

Nicole Kidman is probably Australia's best-known contemporary film star. Others cinematic high fliers include Judy Davis, Geoffrey Rush (winner of the 1997 best actor Oscar for *Shine*) and the great swashbuckler Errol Flynn, who hailed from Tasmania. New Zealand-born Russell Crowe – who won the 2001 best actor Oscar for *Gladiator* – lives in Australia when he's not making movies, and Mel Gibson grew up in Australia.

Founded at the end of the 19th century, the Australian film industry took a great leap forward in the 1970s and has never really looked back. Films such as *Picnic at Hanging Rock*, *My Brilliant Career*, *Breaker Morant*, the *Mad Max* series and *Crocodile Dundee* – as well as the more off-beat *Strictly Ballroom* and *The Adventures of Priscilla, Queen of the Desert* – have given audiences around the world a glimpse of Australia's scenery and perhaps provided insight into the national character and preoccupations. *The Piano* and *Muriel's Wedding* also excelled. Multi-screen cinema complexes are popular in town centres as well as suburbs. Big cities also have specialised cinemas showing art films, foreign films and revivals.

SHOPPING

In most cities, the browsers and window-shoppers congregate along the pedestrian malls. Department-store chains such as David Jones, Grace Bros and Myer provide a dependable cross-section of what's available. Downtown arcades and courts are crammed with smaller boutiques handling everything from high fashion to silly souvenirs.

In Sydney the skyscrapers have subterranean shopping arcades; the Queen Victoria Building by Town Hall station is a great place to browse. In Melbourne the main shopping streets are Collins and Bourke, along with the Bourke Street Mall. Rundle Mall is the essence of shopping in Adelaide, and traffic-free Hay Street Mall is Perth's sprawling equivalent.

Shopping hours usually run nonstop from 8.30 or 9am to 5 or 5.30pm, Monday to Friday, and to 5pm on Saturdays in major towns and cities. One night a week, either Thursday or Friday depending on the city, the stores stay open until 9pm or thereabouts. In larger cities, tourist needs are catered for on Sundays as well. Some big-city stores operate 24

Many of Sydney's shopping streets are pedestrianised

hours a day. Here's a brief survey of the distinctive shopping possibilities to keep in mind as you travel across Australia.

Aboriginal Arts and Crafts

Some good places to find authentic boomerangs, didgeridoos and works of art are the Northern Territory and North Queensland, but you can find Aboriginal products in speciality stores all over the country. Outback artists produce traditional paintings on bark, the subjects and style recalling the prehistoric rock paintings featuring kangaroos, emus, fish, snakes, crocodiles and impressions of tribal ceremonies. Other indigenous painters use modern materials to produce canvases in a style that looks uncannily like some abstract-expressionist work, yet recounting Dreamtime legends and rituals. Though the themes are old, the economics are contemporary: the price tags on paintings may go into four or even five figures.

Fine workmanship is also seen on some of the painted wood sculptures of animals and birds. You'll see large, brightly decorated didgeridoos – indigenous wind instruments made from tree trunks hollowed out by obliging termites. Slightly easier to transport are clap-sticks for percussion accompaniment. Some Aboriginal craftsmen also produce decorated wooden shields and, rather inevitably, boomerangs. Baskets and table-mats woven from pandanus leaves are perhaps easier to carry home.

A word of warning: fakes and kitsch are sometimes represented as Aboriginal art by unscrupulous traders. To help

A collection of didgeridoos in traditional Aboriginal colours

identify genuine Aboriginal and Torres Strait Islander art, cultural products and services, Aboriginal communities have developed the Label of Authenticity, which employs the Aboriginal colours black, red and yellow and is protected by law.

Art and Antiques

Paintings and prints by contemporary Australian artists are on show in commercial galleries in many areas, but the biggest concentration is in the big cities. Sydney galleries are clustered in the central shopping district and in Paddington. In Melbourne visit the City, Toorak Road and High Street, Armadale. They'll handle the packing, insurance and shipping details for you.

Antiques include some worthy colonial pieces: furniture, clocks, jewellery, porcelain, silverware, glassware and maps. Some dealers specialise in non-Australian antiques, for instance Chinese ceramics or Japanese screens. In Sydney, the Paddington district is full of antiques shops. Melbourne's antiques centre is High Street, Armadale.

Huon pine, a slow-growing conifer unique to Tasmania, has long attracted the attention of wood-carvers. The timber, which is heavy, fine-grained and perfumed, is carved into furniture, salad bowls, egg-cups, candlesticks and even hair-curlers. If there's no room for a carved artefact in your luggage, you can buy sachets of sweet-scented Huon pine shavings, to breathe in when you feel nostalgic for Tassie.

Clothing

The **fashion** season just ending in Australia is always about to begin north of the equator – so Australian end-of-season sales can deliver excellent bargains that are instantly wearable upon your return home. 'Wearable art' in swimwear, fashion garments, fabrics and souvenirs proliferates. Names to look for include Ken Done, Desert Designs, Balarinji Australia, Country Road, Covers, Trent Nathan, Lizzie Collins, Studibaker Hawk, Perri Cutten, Von Troska, Alannah Hill, Jodie Boffa, Scanlan and Theodore, Morissey Edmiston, Collette Dinnigan, Saba and Robert Burton.

A distinct style of **Outback clothing** has evolved from rural Australia, the area collectively known as 'The Bush'. Driza-bone oilskin raincoats, Akubra hats (wide-brimmed hats that are usually made of felt) and the R.M. Williams range of bush wear (including boots and moleskin trousers) are good examples.

Typical Australian felt hats: dangling corks are optional

Consider a pair of Blundstone boots, made in Tasmania and renowned for their durability.

Sheepskin: In a country where sheep outnumber humans by ten to one, their hides are manufactured into a wide range of items. If it isn't too hot to think about it, you can choose from sheepskin boots, hats, coats, rugs and novelty items.

Woollen goods: It's those sheep again: Look for high-quality sweaters and scarves, and tapestries, too. You can also buy hand-spun wool. Australian merino sheep produce fine fleece ideally suited for spinning. All kinds of knitwear, from vivid children's clothing to Jumbuk brand greasy wool sweaters (which retain their natural water resistance) are available.

Precious Stones

Australia is the source of about 95 percent of the world's **opals**. 'White' opals are mined from the fields of Andamooka and Coober Pedy in South Australia, where inhabitants live underground to escape searing summer heat. 'Boulder' opals – bright and vibrant – come from Quilpie in Queensland, while the precious 'black' opal (actually more blue than black) is mined at Lightning Ridge and White Cliffs in New South Wales. Opals, considered among Australia's best buys, are sold unset or as finished jewellery. Larger jewellery shops can arrange duty-free purchase for foreign visitors, but you may have to pay duty when you arrive home. The products are virtually unrivalled anywhere else in the world.

After opals, **sapphires** are Australia's most-mined gemstones. A sapphire is exactly the same stone as a ruby – the only difference is the name and the colour. Creative Australian jewellers work wonders with sapphires.

Diamonds are mined by Argyle Diamond Mines in the rugged Kimberley region in the country's west; Australia is one of the world's largest diamond sources. The Kimberley is famed for its 'pink' diamonds, sometimes marketed under the description 'champagne'. Hues range from lightly flushed to deep red.

Souvenirs

Souvenirs, whether ingenious or hackneyed, indigenous or imported, pop up everywhere you travel: in cities, resorts and along the way at roadside stands. Tourists seem unable to resist miniature kangaroos, koalas and,

Australia's major museums all have gift shops, and many of them sell specially commissioned items, such as reproduction artworks or Aboriginal artefacts, that cannot be bought elsewhere.

in Tasmania, almost-lovable Tasmanian devil dolls.

A selection of plastic boomerangs and beer can-holders head the very long list of less artistic souvenirs, followed by saucy T-shirts. In Sydney, you'll find them cheap at Paddy's Market. In Melbourne, try Queen Victoria Market.

Kangaroo-skin souvenirs include toy kangaroos and koalas and other such products – some of them are quite trite. The cheapest of

Wear a marsupial on your T-shirt

the stuffed kangaroos and koalas, often wrapped up in patriotic Australian packaging, are imported. One widespread and distinctly Aussie item is the kangaroo-scrotum purse – a must for the collector of bad-taste souvenirs. Look out, too, for fashion accessories such as brooches and earrings made from coconuts.

Duty-free Shopping

This is highly organised throughout Australia, not just at airports but also in the cities. Regulations require the duty-free chains to offer goods in their downtown outlets at the same price as at their airport shops, where you can save up to 30 percent on jewellery, watches, electrical goods, cameras, alcohol etc. You will be required to produce your air ticket and passport at the duty-free store; you mustn't open the packages before you leave the country; and on your departure you are obliged to show them to the customs agent – who will be looking for you.

Calendar of Events

January

- First Wine in the World Celebration, Chateau Hornsby Winery, Alice Springs: Early on 1 January, watch as the shiraz grapes are made into the 'early red', the first wine of the year anywhere in the world.
- Sydney Festival: a month of concerts, drama, exhibitions, sport etc.
- Perth Cup: horse racing classic at Royal Ascot Racecourse.
- Country Music Festival, Tamworth, New South Wales.
- Australian Tennis Open: Grand Slam event at Melbourne Park.
- Hobart Summer Festival: six-week celebration of culture and food.
- Port Lincoln Tunarama Free Festival: on the foreshore of Boston Bay, South Australia (includes the world tuna-throwing championships).

February

- Perth Festival: sporting and cultural events.
- Adelaide Festival of Arts (even-numbered years): three weeks of opera, ballet, theatre, art and literary events.
- Womadelaide (odd-numbered years): Adelaide's world music festival.
- Launceston Cup: the social event of Tasmania. Much more than just a horse race, it is the culmination of a one-month racing programme.

March–April

- Sydney Gay and Lesbian Mardi Gras Parade: fun-filled, provocative parade along Oxford Street.
- Australian Grand Prix: Formula 1 racing at Albert Park, Melbourne.
- Moomba Festival, Melbourne: carnival with fireworks, music, river pageants and a street parade.
- Canberra National Multicultural Festival.
- South Australia Vintage Festival, Barossa Valley (odd-numbered years): celebrating the wine harvest with German-Australian gaiety.
- Sydney Royal Easter Show, near Olympic Park.
- Sydney Cup Week: a pageant of horse racing.

May

- Barossa Valley Balloon Regatta: Nuriootpa in the Barossa Valley.
- Adelaide Cup: horse race and associated festivities.
- Australian Celtic Festival, New South Wales: dancing, singing and art.

June

- Darwin Beer Can Regatta: all the boats constructed of used beer cans.
- A Taste of Manly: Sydney's largest annual food and wine festival.
- Bounty Day, Norfolk Island: 8 June (anniversary of the *Bounty* mutineers' arrival in 1856), festivities culminate in a Bounty Ball.
- Brisbane Cup: horse race.

July

- Camel Cup: camel racing at Blatherskite Park, Alice Springs.
- Gold Coast Marathon: Queensland.
- Melbourne Grand National: steeplechase.
- Royal Darwin Show: agricultural exhibition.

August–September

- Royal Queensland Show, Brisbane: agricultural fair with fireworks.
- Mount Isa Rodeo and Festival, Queensland: Australia's biggest rodeo.
- Henley-on-Todd Regatta, Alice Springs: dry-land bottomless boat race.
- Australian Masters Alpine Ski Races: Snowy Mountains.
- Royal Adelaide Show: South Australia's agricultural summit meeting.
- Royal Melbourne Show: bucolic and sporting attractions.
- Carnival of Flowers: Toowoomba, Queensland.
- Birdsville Races, Queensland: a weekend of horse racing and revelry.
- Floriade, Canberra: Australia's biggest flower show.
- Jabiru Wind Festival: cultural community event in Kakadu National Park.

October

- Melbourne International Festival: visual and performing arts.
- Australian Motorcycle Grand Prix: Phillip Island, Victoria.
- Royal Hobart Agricultural Show: Tasmania's agricultural highlight.

November

- Melbourne Cup: one of the world's premier horse-racing events.
- Sydney Sleaze Ball: themed gay and lesbian party.

December

- Western Australian Turf Club Derby: horse racing.
- Sydney–Hobart: one of the world's toughest yacht races.
- Various capital cities: New Year's Eve Celebrations with fireworks are gigantic, festive affairs.

EATING OUT

If you enjoy dining out at bargain prices, with a wide choice of menus reflecting varied ethnic influences, you're going to enjoy mealtimes in Australia's cities. Eating well in the land down under doesn't carry an inflated price tag. The whole country is well stocked with inexpensive bistros, cafés and food markets where diverse and wholesome cuisine can be enjoyed at moderate prices. Current exchange rates with major world currencies make Australia even more of a gastronomic bargain.

All state capitals have a lively café scene and most support 'BYO'. The initials stand for 'bring your own' and allow you to take along store-bought wine to enjoy with your meal. Australian wine is relatively inexpensive and of high quality – you can buy it at pubs or from a wide variety of discount liquor outlets. Many other restaurants are licensed, with their own wine cellars.

The average urban-dwelling Australian eats out several times a week – a testimony to the quality and affordability of the food. In the words of Barbara Kafka, one of America's foremost food writers and cookbook authors, 'Australians have one of the most extraordinary assortments of basic ingredients of high quality anywhere in the world, and at exceptionally modest prices.'

On a visit in 1996, renowned chef and gourmet Robert Carrier went into raptures: 'I've never had such tastes, such subtleties, such delights, such form, such colour,' he told Australian *Gourmet Traveller* magazine. At least half a dozen restaurateurs, if they set up in Paris, would be instant successes, Carrier declared.

Australian cooks have the advantage of the availability of a wonderful palette of ingredients. The country's climatic diversity provides a wide range of fresh vegetables and fruits, ranging from exotic rambutans, coconuts and lychees to apples and spinach.

This culinary wonderland is relatively new. During most of the two centuries of modern Australia's existence, its inhabitants subsisted on bland 'meat and veg' fodder. Cultural intermingling since World War II has revolutionised the national diet. Urban Australia now eats what has been described as 'fusion food' – a collage of culinary influences that enlivens basic fish, grain or meat with, for example, a handful of chopped coriander, a splash of olive oil and a dash of chilli.

Indigenous Cuisine

Recent innovations by Australian chefs have included greater use of indigenous foods in fine dining. Lemon aspen, bush tomatoes, Illawarra plums, lemon myrtle, lilli pillies, muntari berries and other mysterious ingredients are now appearing on menus, often blended with traditional dishes of meat and fish. Kangaroo and emu are commercially farmed and processed. (Both meats are low in fat and high in fibre.) Collectively known as native food – or sometimes bush tucker – these are just some of the fruits, seeds, nuts, fungi, mammals, reptiles, fish and birds that sustained Australia's indigenous inhabitants for up to 100,000 years before white settlers came to the region. Other bush-tucker ingredients include quandongs (similar to a peach with a touch of rhubarb), wattle seeds (sometimes used in ice cream), Kakadu plums (less sweet than the usual variety) and bunya bunya nuts (delicious in satay). Even wilder Aboriginal ingredients, not yet widespread in restaurants, include the Bogong moth (a hefty moth roasted in a fire and eaten like a peanut) and the witchetty grub (a puffy, white grub found in the trunks and roots of certain wattle trees). The witchetty grub has been shown to be a virtual powerhouse of protein.

If you're into exotic fare, sample goat cheeses from Western Australia, cold-pressed olive oils from South Australia, buffalo mozzarella from New South Wales, or oysters, salmon and other seafood ingredients from Tasmania.

The gastronomic revolution has yet to take hold in most working-class suburbs, or in rural areas. A typical menu in a small-town café

Seafood-lovers are spoilt for choice in Australia

will probably include nothing more exotic than *moussaka* or spaghetti bolognese. The traditional Aussie meat pie, doused liberally with tomato sauce, rules supreme in these outposts, as does the hamburger. Outside the standardised US chains, Australian hamburgers tend to include beetroot and lettuce rather than pickle.

What to Eat

Breakfast is anything you want it to be, from muesli and grapes or coffee and croissant to a full cooked meal. It depends on where you are and your hunger level. If you are really starving, some establishments will serve you a breakfast based on steak or lamb chops with eggs. It's also possible to find original oddities such as spaghetti on toast.

Fish and seafood. From traditional fish and chips eaten standing up to lobster savoured by candlelight, Australia's temperate and tropical oceans offer a fantastic choice of seafood. Fish adorning the menu include the delicious snapper, the meaty John Dory, smallish flounder and bigger sole, the bony but flavoursome whiting (no relation to the English whiting) and the tropical trevally. Then there's barramundi, which means 'big scales' in an Aboriginal language, and is found in both fresh and salt water; game fishermen in the north take 'barra' of up to 15kg (33lb). Along the Great Barrier Reef they even eat red emperor, a fish so gorgeous it might take a snorkeller's breath away.

Treat yourself to succulent seafood specialities such as Sydney rock oysters, as delicious as any in the world, and Brisbane's famous Moreton Bay bug, a crustacean to gloat over, and gloriously meaty mud crabs. Lobster, grilled or thermidor, is priced for special occasions. You are also likely to come across some of the lobster's freshwater cousins, small crayfish known locally as yabbies. Prices are less forbidding when it comes to steamed mussels or prawns. A popular and simple Australian alfresco meal for two consists of a kilo (2.2lb) of prawns and a bottle of ice-cold white wine. Scrumptious!

Meat favourites include steak and roast lamb, particularly in the simpler restaurants. Steak will be served well done unless you specify 'rare' or 'blue' (really rare). If you feel up to it, try a 'carpetbag steak' (stuffed with oysters). Meat pies, a long-established staple, vary according to region: in Adelaide the speciality is the 'floater', a pie served floating in pea soup. You can even dine on kangaroo or emu if you're feeling adventurous.

Vegetables are available in as much variety as anywhere else in the world, but some restaurants prefer to serve meat dishes with salad – mainly because it doesn't require cooking and is easier to prepare. If you want vegetables, ask for them. Many Australian chefs are willing to accommodate customer requests.

Fruit in Australia covers all the climatic zones. To name a few: the more familiar apples, cherries, plums and berries from the temperate latitudes; and tropical avocados, bananas, papayas, passion fruit, pineapples and mangoes.

Desserts. You'll be able to find as many as you might want. A traditional Australian favourite is the light and fluffy pavlova, a meringue concoction traditionally topped with kiwi fruit. It's a little unfashionable these days, but worth sampling if you can get it. Peach Melba, named after Melbourne's most famous opera singer Nellie Melba, is still frequently found on dessert menus – and not just in Melbourne.

Exotic Imports

The massive migration from Mediterranean countries after World War II made the first real dent in Australia's monolithic Anglo-Saxon palate. Italians in particular helped revolutionise cooking, introducing wary Aussies to the wonders of pasta, garlic and olive oil. Today, each capital city has its concentration of Italian restaurants – Melbourne's Lygon Street and Sydney's Leichhardt district being the most famous –

The elegant Café Panache in Fremantle, Western Australia

serving authentic, well-priced food. In Melbourne, with its large Greek population, it is easy to find traditionally made *taramasalata*, *dolmades* or *souvlaki*.

That was only the beginning. The extension of immigration in the 1970s added myriad new cuisines. The great melting-pot of Australian society meant that restaurants were suddenly opened by Lebanese, Turkish, Balkan, Hungarian and Spanish chefs.

But the biggest impact by far has been made by the Asians. Regional Chinese, Thai, Vietnamese, Japanese and Indian restaurants are now Australia's biggest success stories, with Korean, Sri Lankan, Singaporean and Indonesian cuisines waiting in the wings. Every capital city offers pristine *teppanyaki* dining rooms and take-away *lakhsa* stalls. Singapore-style 'food courts' have sprung up, with several fast-food stalls offering meals from different Asian coun-

Pinot Noir is one of the European grapes grown successfully in Australia

tries. Even local supermarkets now stock the required pastes and condiment's for everyones favourite Thai or Indian dish.

Australian Wines

The wines of Australia are among the world's best – a judgment confirmed consistently at international wine shows. Not only are the country's finest wines world-beaters, but even the humble 'kangarouge' sold in boxes ('casks') is the worthy equivalent of any *vin de table* served in a bistro in France. Australians drink twice as much wine per capita as Americans or Britons, and anything that's left over (100 million litres of it) is exported to over 80 countries. Wine is one of the country's most important export industries and the range sold in liquor stores is extensive and moderately priced.

Australia's interest in wine production stretches back a couple of centuries. The founder of the New South Wales colony, Captain Arthur Phillip certainly had his priorities right, and one of the first projects he ordered in 1788 was the planting of vines at Sydney Cove. Because of factors such as the damp and the sea breezes, the site (now part of Sydney's Botanic Gardens) was quite wrong for growing grapes, which developed 'black spot', and the experiment failed. But in 1791 three acres of vines were successfully planted a few miles inland.

Rum, rather than wine, became the favourite drink under Governor Phillip's successor. Free-enterprising army officers enjoyed a monopoly on the staggeringly profitable sales of rum, and widespread abuses were reported to London. It was Captain William Bligh, the original hardliner of *Bounty* fame, who was dispatched to clean up Australia. Governor Bligh was deposed in the Rum Rebellion of 1808, a mutiny led by one of the first wine-growers, John Macarthur.

Today, most of Australia's European grape varieties are grown by some 930 wineries in 75,000 hectares (185,000 acres) of vineyards. Riesling, Chardonnay and Semillon are the most favoured white varieties, while popular reds include Cabernet Sauvignon, Pinot Noir and Shiraz (also known in Europe as Syrah). Climatic conditions ranging from warm to hot provide excellent ripening, with an abundance of flavour and comparatively high alcohol levels. Australia's vintage (harvest) occurs between January and May each year.

Wine is produced in every state, even temperate Tasmania and the baking hot Northern Territory (where a small 'chateau' holds forth on the edge of Alice Springs). The biggest producer is South Australia, where the best-known wineries are situated in the beautiful Barossa Valley. The most important wine-producing region of New South Wales is the Hunter Valley. Victoria boasts numerous wine-growing regions, and Western Australia's Swan Valley and Margaret River areas have also made their mark.

If you're interested in seeing where the wine comes from, every state capital has wine-growing areas nearby, and the chance to sample wines at the cellar door is one of their best features. As the majority of wineries are concentrated in a relatively small area, they make ideal touring for a day or – better still – two days, either independently or on a guided tour.

Downing the amber nectar in a Port Douglas pub

The Amber Nectar

Melbourne was the centre of a brewing revolution 100 years ago. During the 19th century, most Australian beer was made like English ales, until lighter Continental-style lagers were brewed in Melbourne by German immigrants. Nowadays lager is the dominant style, and it's hugely popular throughout the country. The citizens of Darwin drink more beer per capita than anyone else in the world. The 'Darwin Stubby' is reputedly the world's largest bottle of beer, containing 2¼ litres (nearly a gallon).

In Darwin they drink more beer than anywhere else in the world

Beer in Australia is served very cold. Low temperature is considered so important that beer-lovers will insist on glasses that have been chilled, or will keep their 'tinnie' (can of beer) in an insulating jacket.

Australia's best-known beer is probably Fosters lager, but that's only one of many varieties. Reschs, Tooheys, Victoria Bitter, Castlemaine xxxx, Swan and Cascade are also popular brands. Some beers are sold in 'new' and 'old' types, the first being lager and the latter darker in colour. Coopers beer, made in South Australia, is a favourite among connoisseurs – it's rich and strong, similar to the best British real ales.

Australia's standard alcoholic strength for canned beer is 4.9 percent – pretty strong by international standards. A word of advice for weight-watchers from Europe or America: the word 'light' or 'lite' applied to beer in Australia means lighter in alcohol, not lighter in calories. It has exactly the same calorific content as the regular type. The alcoholic strength of Australian beer must by law be displayed on the can or bottle.

HANDY TRAVEL TIPS

An A–Z summary of practical information

A

ACCOMMODATION (see also CAMPING, YOUTH HOSTELS)

Australia welcomes the traveller with all kinds of accommodation. The luxury end of the spectrum matches the most sumptuous world standards, in the rooms and suites as well as the associated restaurants, lounges, saunas and spas. But even in budget-priced hotel and motel rooms you can expect a private shower or bath and toilet, a telephone, a TV set, a small refrigerator and coffee and tea-making equipment (and free coffee, tea and milk). In most areas air-conditioning, or at least a ceiling fan, is provided.

There's no limit to the level of luxury a hotel or motel can attain, and either type can be anywhere – along the highway or right downtown. Distinguishing between the two can be confusing. The only sure difference is that a hotel has a bar open to the public – indeed, the most modest ones have little else to offer. To add to the confusion, 'hotel' is also a synonym for 'pub' here. If a motel has a bar, it's usually strictly for the guests. You simply can't judge a hostelry by what it calls itself.

Private hotels, often small guesthouses, do not have a licence for alcohol. Bed-and-breakfast establishments – private homes taking paying guests – exist in towns or out on the farms. Big towns and resorts also have self-catering apartments with maid service and fully equipped kitchens, convenient for longer stays.

Overseas offices of the Australian Tourist Commission have listings of hotels and motels – website <www.australia.com>. You can reserve accommodation through your travel agent, the nearest offices of the international and Australian hotel chains, or your airline. Within Australia, the state tourist bureaux, domestic airlines and hotel chains offer instant free bookings. If you arrive out of the blue, local tourist offices have desks for last-minute reservations.

Accommodation may be hard to find when Australians themselves go travelling by the million, during school holidays. These can vary, but most states have adopted a four-term school year with two-week breaks in April, June/July and September/October. The Christmas/summer holidays are from mid-December to the beginning of February.

AIRPORTS

The principal gateways are Sydney, Melbourne, Brisbane, Darwin and Perth. Other international airports serve Adelaide, Townsville, Hobart and Cairns. The domestic air network is very well developed, and even smallish towns usually have comfortable, efficient terminals. The biggest airports have the full range of restaurants and bars, newsstands, souvenir shops, post office and banks. The international airports have duty-free shops for both arriving and departing passengers.

Arriving passengers can travel from airport to town by taxi or bus. In Sydney, Brisbane, Adelaide, Darwin and Perth, airport bus services go to and from the door of most hotels. Travel time ranges from 20 minutes (Perth and Darwin) to 40 minutes (Sydney). Note that Sydney Airport's domestic and international terminals are a shuttle-bus ride apart. There's also a rail link between Sydney Airport and Sydney Central Station.

Check-in time for departing passengers on domestic flights is one hour before the scheduled flight time; international flights require check-in at least two hours in advance.

B

BICYCLE HIRE

Most Australian cities are reasonably attuned to cyclists, and bicycle lanes are sometimes marked on inner-city streets. Cars clog large cities, however, and attempts to cater for cyclists are often little more than cosmetic. Canberra is an exception; cycling there is excellent. Throughout Australia, by law cyclists must wear helmets at all times.

Organised cycle tours of varying lengths are available, including transport to and from a scenic area (bikes provided), food and accommodation. You can also rent touring bikes. For details, look up 'Bicycles & Accessories – Retail & Repairs' in the Yellow Pages phone book of the relevant city. Local cycling organisations are a good source of information:

Bicycle Federation of Australia, tel: (03) 9827 4453 <www.bfa. asn.au>.

Pedal Power ACT (Canberra), tel: (02) 6248 7995 <www.sunsite. anu.edu.au.community/pedalpower>.

Bicycle New South Wales, tel: (02) 9283 5200 <www.bicyclensw. org.au>.

Bicycle Queensland, tel: (07) 3844 1144 <www.uq.net.au/~zzbikeq>.

Bicycle Institute of South Australia, tel: (08) 8271 5824 <www. bisa.asn.au>.

Bicycle Victoria, tel: (03) 9328 3000 <www.bv.com.au>.

BUDGETING FOR YOUR TRIP

You can eat out well for little money: a plate of noodles or pasta can cost A$8 or less. Exchange rates have shifted in favour of major foreign currencies in recent years, boosting the value even further.

Accommodation also represents good value when measured against equivalents in other developed countries. Air travel is a relatively high-ticket item, but the arrival of two new challengers on domestic air routes – Virgin Blue and Impulse Airlines – has triggered periodic spates of fare discounting. International passengers may be entitled to discounted travel within Australia, depending on the airline they arrive on and their fare type. International fares to Australia have fallen steadily in real terms over the past decade.

On the ground, train travel can be competitive for shorter distances, and budget long-distance coach operations abound.

Inflation in Australia has remained low since the early 1990s. In 2002, the cost of a litre of petrol (gasoline) was approximately A$1 – more expensive than in the US but cheaper than in most European countries.

C

CAMPING (see also CAR HIRE AND NATIONAL PARKS)

Australians are avid campers, and you'll find campsites dotted all over the areas frequented by tourists. The sites tend to be jam-packed at school holiday times. They have at least the basic amenities, and in some cases much more in the way of comfort. Apart from roomy tents with lights and floors, some installations have caravans (trailers) or cabins for rent. Showers, toilets, laundry facilities and barbecue grills are commonly available.

The national parks generally have well-organised camping facilities; to camp beyond the designated zone you must ask the rangers for permission. There are coach tours for campers, or you can rent a camper van or motorhome by the day or week.

CAR HIRE (see also DRIVING)

For seeing the Australian countryside at your own pace, there's no substitute for a car. Brisk competition among the international and local car hire companies means you can often find economical rates or special deals, for instance unlimited mileage or weekend discounts. Rates are considerably higher if you drive in remote country areas. In general, it's worth shopping around. But be careful – some cheap companies impose a metropolitan limit on vehicles. Check first, as your insurance won't be valid outside the designated area.

In busy locations you can hire anything from a super-economy model or a four-wheel-drive vehicle to a limousine with or without chauffeur. Campervans and caravans are available, though many are reserved well in advance for school holiday periods.

To hire a car you'll need a current Australian, overseas or International Driving Licence. The minimum age is 21, or in some cases 25. Third-party insurance is automatically included, and for an additional fee you can also sign up for collision damage waiver and personal accident insurance.

You can pick up a car in one city and return it elsewhere. Interstate arrangements are commonly available from the big firms like Avis <www.avis.com/au>, Hertz <www.hertz.com.au>, Thrifty <www.thrifty.com.au> and Budget <www.budget.com.au>, which also have offices at airports.

CLIMATE

Travellers from the Northern Hemisphere find Australia's seasons upside down: winter runs from June to August and Christmas comes in summertime. But it's much more complicated than that, for Australia covers so much ground, from the tropics to the temperate zone.

From November to March it's mostly hot, or at least quite warm, everywhere. In the north this period brings the rains, which can wash out roads and otherwise spoil holiday plans. In the south the nights, at least, are mild. April to September is generally ideal in the tropics and central Australia – clear and warm. Occasional rain refreshes the south, with snow in the southern mountains.

For your guidance, the table below gives the average daily maximum and minimum temperatures in degrees Fahrenheit. (Minimum temperatures are measured just before sunrise, maximum temperatures in the afternoon.)

		J	F	M	A	M	J	J	A	S	O	N	D
Sydney	max.	79	77	77	72	66	63	61	63	68	72	75	77
	min.	64	64	63	59	52	48	46	48	52	55	59	63
Brisbane	max.	84	84	82	79	73	71	68	72	75	79	82	84
	min.	69	68	66	61	55	52	48	50	55	61	64	63
Alice	max.	99	97	91	84	73	68	66	72	79	88	93	95
Springs	min.	72	71	64	57	48	43	41	45	50	59	64	68
Perth	max.	86	86	82	75	71	64	63	64	66	71	77	81
	min.	64	64	63	57	54	50	48	48	50	52	57	61

...and the same in degrees Celsius:

		J	F	M	A	M	J	J	A	S	O	N	D
Sydney	max.	26	25	25	22	19	17	16	17	20	22	24	25
	min.	18	18	17	15	11	9	8	9	11	13	15	17
Brisbane	max.	29	29	28	26	23	21	20	22	24	26	28	29
	min.	21	20	19	16	13	11	9	10	13	16	18	17
Alice	max.	37	36	33	29	23	20	19	22	26	31	34	35
Springs	min.	22	21	18	14	9	6	5	7	10	15	18	20
Perth	max.	30	30	28	24	21	18	17	18	19	21	25	27
	min.	18	18	17	14	12	10	9	9	10	11	14	16

By way of regional superlatives, Darwin is the state capital with the highest average hours of sunshine, but it also gets the most rain. Adelaide has the lowest average rainfall of all capital cities. Far to the south, Hobart is the coolest capital; its climate is similar to that of Britain. But statistics indicate that the cities of Australia bask in more sunshine than any others in the world.

CLOTHING

A sweater may come in handy, even in summer. After a hot day in the sun, the evening breeze can seem downright chilly. A light raincoat will serve in any season. Anywhere you go you'll need comfortable walking shoes. Because of the strong sun, a hat is advisable – particularly in the Outback.

While Sydneysiders dress casually at weekends (shorts, a short-sleeved shirt or T-shirt and trainers or sandals are perfect), business attire can be surprisingly conservative. Visit any popular downtown pub in Sydney or Melbourne at lunchtime on a summer weekday and you encounter hundreds of men in dark blue suits and ties, trying to cope with the sweltering heat. Sydney has yet to adapt fully to its climate and adopt the open-necked informality seen in many warm countries. Restaurants have dropped the requirement for men to wear jacket and tie, but some establishments may refuse customers wearing T-shirts, tank tops or ripped jeans. Entering clubs generally requires a collared shirt and covered shoes – no trainers or sandals.

COMPLAINTS

If you think you've been overcharged or unfairly dealt with, the personal approach can be effective in plain-talking Australia. If not, consider contacting the travel agency that made the booking. Failing that, phone or write to the Department of Fair Trading or Department of Consumer Affairs in the Australian state or territory concerned. Their contact details are listed in the phone book's White Pages, up front in the government section.

CRIME AND SAFETY (see also EMERGENCIES)

As in most countries, it's wise to take precautions against burglary and petty theft. Check your valuables into the hotel's safe deposit box. Lock your room and your car. Be alert for pickpockets on crowded buses and in the markets.

Overall, Australia is a safe place. Sydney's murder rate (two per 100,000 citizens) is low by world standards and the city, Australia's biggest, has a relatively low crime rate. The same is true of other Australian cities, although muggings and fights are not unknown. It's best to avoid city parks after dark, particularly if on your own. Anti-drug laws vary greatly from state to state. Possession of small amounts of cannabis for personal use is generally either overlooked or dealt with by a fine. Narcotics are treated much more severely.

CUSTOMS AND ENTRY REQUIREMENTS

Australia is the only country in the developed world to require all visitors to hold a visa. Citizens of New Zealand (which enjoys strong historical links with Australia) receive an automatic electronic visa when they present their passports at the Immigration desk.

Australia's Electronic Travel Authority (ETA), allows travel agents to issue an 'invisible visa' electronically to visitors at time of booking in their home countries. Tourists or travellers visiting friends or relatives and wishing to stay for up to three months on each visit within a 12-month period should apply for the Tourist ETA (Type V), which is issued free. Those making a business visit should inquire whether they require a type BL or type BS visa.

The ETA eliminates having to find an embassy or consulate. The process can be completed in person or over the phone. This has greatly shortened the time most passengers have to wait at airport Customs and Immigration desks. You can apply for a visa allowing multiple travel for up to four years, with a stay of three to six months on each visit. An application fee is then payable.

If you wish to extend your stay beyond three months, you will need to contact the nearest office of the Department of Immigration and Multicultural Affairs in Australia before the end of your three-month stay. ETAS are currently available to citizens of Andorra, Austria, Belgium, Brunei, Canada, Denmark, Finland, France, Germany, Greece, Iceland, Ireland, Italy, Japan, Liechtenstein, Luxembourg, Malaysia, Malta, Monaco, Netherlands, Norway, Singapore, South Korea, Spain, Sweden, Switzerland, UK, US and Vatican City. The list is growing. The department's web sites <www.immi.gov.au> and <www.dima.gov.au> have the latest information.

Australia operates reciprocal working holiday programmes with countries including Canada, Ireland, Japan, Korea, Malta, the Netherlands and the UK, for applicants between 18 and 25 (and in special circumstances, 26 to 30), either single or married without children. Working holiday visas allow recipients to work for up to three months at a time, over a one-year period.

On arrival in Australia, you may have to show your return or onward ticket, and prove that you have sufficient funds for your stay. On entry, you may take into Australia duty-free up to one litre (2 pints) of alcohol and 250 cigarettes or 250g (9oz) of tobacco.

D

DRIVING (see also CAR HIRE)

Road Conditions

Australian roads are good considering the size of the country and the challenges of distance, terrain and climate. Freeways link populous regions, but most country roads are two-lane highways, which can be crowded at busy times.

Rules and Regulations

Australians drive on the left – which means the steering wheel is on the right, and you overtake on the right. Drivers and passengers must wear seat belts. (The exception is buses, although many of them feature seat belts as an option.) Car-hire companies can supply suitable child restraints, boosters and baby seats at an extra charge.

A tourist may drive in Australia on a valid overseas licence for the same class of vehicle. Licences must always be carried when driving. If the licence is in a language other than English, the visitor must carry a translation with the licence. An International Driver's Permit is not sufficient by itself and must be accompanied by a valid national driver's licence.

The speed limit in cities and towns is generally 60kph (about 35mph) but sometimes is cut to 40kph (about 25mph). Outside built-up areas the speed limit is generally either 100kph or 110kph (about 70mph). There is no speed limit outside of built-up areas in the Northern Territory.

Throughout Australia, police make random checks for drugs or alcohol, using breath tests. The limit on alcohol in the blood is generally about 0.05, meaning in practice that three glasses of wine or three half-pint glasses of beer in an hour will take you to the limit. In New South Wales, if you are under 25 and in your first three years of driving, you must be under 0.02, which doesn't allow you to drink at all. In any state, being over the limit means an automatic hefty fine.

Outback Driving

Check thoroughly the condition of your car and be sure you have a spare tyre and plenty of spare drinking water. Find out about the fuel situation in advance and always be sure to leave word as to your destination and anticipated arrival time. Fill up the fuel tank at every opportunity, for the next station may be a few hundred kilometres away. Some dirt roads are so smooth you may be tempted to speed, but conditions can change abruptly. Be cautious when you encounter a 'road train' – a high-powered truck towing three or four huge trailers along the highway at speed. Pass them only with the greatest of care.

Parking

Heavy traffic and parking problems afflict some downtown areas. Parking meters and 'no standing' zones are everywhere, so be careful where you leave the car.

If you need help

The Automobile Association <www.aaa.asn.au> is a national body that maintains links with similar organisations worldwide. Many state automobile associations have reciprocal arrangements with similar organisations overseas, so bring proof of your membership.

New South Wales: NMRA, 388 George Street, Sydney, NSW 2000; tel: (02) 9292 9222; <www.nrma.com.au>.

Victoria: RACV, 550 Princes Highway, Noble Park, Victoria 3174; tel: (03) 9790 2211; <www.racv.com.au>.

Queensland: RACQ, 300 St Pauls Terrace, Fortitude Valley, Queensland 4006; tel: (07) 3361 2444; <www.racq.com.au>.

South Australia: RAA, 41 Hindmarsh Square, Adelaide, SA 5000; tel: (08) 8202 4500; <www.raa.net>.

Tasmania: RACT, Corner of Patrick and Murray Streets, Hobart, Tasmania 7000; tel: (03) 6232 6300; <www.ract.com.au>.

Western Australia: RACWA, 228 Adelaide Terrace, Perth, WA 6000; tel: (08) 9421 4444; <www.rac.com.au>.

Northern Territory: AANT, 79-81 Smith Street, Darwin, NT 0800; tel: (08) 8981 3837.

Fuel: Some filling stations are open only during normal shopping hours, so you may have to ask where after-hours service is available. Petrol (gasoline) in Australia comes in regular and premium grades, leaded and unleaded, and is sold by the litre. Most stations are self-service and accept international credit cards.

Road Signs: Signs are generally good, especially along heavily used roads. All distances are measured in kilometres. White-on-brown direction signs signal tourist attractions and natural wonders. To drive into the centre of any city, simply follow the signs marked 'City'. Leaving a city is less straightforward: Exit routes are often signposted with the assumption that every driver has local experience, so you may require a good map. Most road signs are the standard international pictographs, but some are unique to Australia, such as large silhouette images of kangaroos or wombats, warning that you may encounter these animals crossing the road. Some signs use words, such as:

Crest steep	hilltop limiting visibility
Cyclist hazard	dangerous for cyclists
Dip	severe depression in road surface
Hump	bump or speed obstacle
Safety ramp	uphill escape lane from steep downhill road

E

ELECTRICITY

The standard throughout Australia is 230–250 volt, 50-cycle AC. Three-pronged plugs, in the shape of a bird's footprint, are universal. They are the same as in New Zealand and many Pacific countries. If you are from elsewhere, you will need an adapter. Many hotel rooms also have 110-volt outlets for razors and small appliances.

EMBASSIES/CONSULATES/HIGH COMMISSIONS

The embassies or high commissions of about 70 countries are established in Canberra, the national capital. They have consular sections dealing with passport renewal, visas and other formalities. Some of them run consular sections in Sydney and other cities, as well. To find the address of your consulate, look in the white pages of the telephone directory under 'Consuls', or in the Yellow Pages under 'Consulates and Legations'.

Here are some of the Canberra embassies and high commissions:

British High Commission (Consular Section): SAP House, Corner of Akuna and Bunda streets, Canberra City, ACT 2601; tel: (02) 6270 6666

Canadian High Commission: Commonwealth Avenue, Yarralumla, ACT 2600; tel: (02) 6270 4000

Irish Embassy: 20 Arkana Street, Yarralumla, ACT 2600; tel: (02) 6273 3022.

Japanese Embassy: 112 Empire Circuit, Yarralumla, ACT 2600; tel: (02) 6273 3244.

New Zealand High Commission: Commonwealth Avenue, Yarralumla, ACT 2600; tel: (02) 6270 4211.

South Africa High Commission: State Circle, Yarralumla, ACT 2600; tel: (02) 6273 2424

United States Embassy: Moonah Place, Yarralumla, ACT 2600; tel: (02) 6214 5600.

EMERGENCIES

Ambulance/Fire/Police: dial 000.

The 000 number – no coin required from public telephones – is in service in all cities and most towns. If you're in a remote area, however, look for the emergency numbers inside the front cover of the telephone directory.

In the big cities there are round-the-clock dental emergency services as well as hospital emergency wards.

G

GAY AND LESBIAN TRAVELLERS

Sydney's popular Gay and Lesbian Mardi Gras has helped make Sydney – and Australia – a popular destination for gay and lesbian travellers. Some tour operators, travel agents and hotels specialise in catering for a gay and lesbian clientele. Australian cities are generally tolerant towards gay and lesbian travellers but prejudice tends to increase in more remote, country areas. Homosexual acts are legal in all states. Sydney is one of the world's major gay cities, sometimes called 'the gay capital of the Southern Hemisphere'. Estimates of its gay population vary, but 400,000 is commonly quoted. Sydney's main gay precinct is Oxford Street (sometimes called 'the Golden Mile') and the surrounding Darlinghurst area, with another precinct in King Street, Newtown.

GETTING TO AUSTRALIA

By Air

Flights from Asia, North America and Europe serve international airports around Australia, including Sydney, Cairns or Melbourne, and you can also fly directly to Darwin, Perth, Brisbane or Adelaide from many international points. Sydney's airport is by far the busiest one in the country. Sydney (and other Australian airports) have particularly high volumes of traffic around the Christmas holiday period, which coincides with the Australian midsummer. Fares are generally at their highest then, and flights are heavily booked in both directions, so it's best to avoid midsummer travel if you are on a budget.

Australia is included in several round-the-world fare constructions – arrangements between two or more airlines which allow passengers to travel globally at bargain rates, provided they complete their journeys within a year and don't backtrack.

Flight times to Sydney (approximate) are London–Sydney 21 hours, New York–Sydney 22 hours, Los Angeles–Sydney 15 hours. You can usually break the flight for a day or two at one of the stops along the way; in most cases this doesn't affect the price of the air ticket.

By Sea
No passenger liners operate to or from Australia any more, but some Australian ports, notably Sydney and Cairns, feature in the itineraries of cruise ships. You can fly to locales like Bali or Singapore and embark on the cruise liner there, sail to Australia, then fly home from any Australian city, or resume the cruise at another port. It tends to be an involved process, however. Travel agents have cruise line schedules and brochures.

GUIDES AND TOURS

Tour companies offer a broad choice of excursions, from a day-trip to Canberra to long-haul journeys into the Outback. There are also local walking tours and tours for cyclists, wildlife-lovers and others catering for special interests.

H

HEALTH AND MEDICAL CARE

Standards of hygiene in Australia are high, particularly in food preparation. Doctors and dentists are proficient and hospitals well-equipped. If you fall ill, your hotel can call a doctor or refer you to one, or you can ask your embassy, high commission or consulate for a list of approved doctors.

You should take out health insurance before departure to cover your stay in Australia. Also ensure that you have personal insurance or travel insurance with a comprehensive health component to cover the possibility of illness or accident.

Medicare, Australia's national health insurance, covers visitors from New Zealand, the UK, Ireland, Malta, Sweden, Italy, Finland

and the Netherlands. To be eligible, contact your national health programme before travelling to Australia to ensure that you have the correct documents to enrol at any Medicare office on arrival in Australia. The agreement provides urgent treatment but doesn't cover elective surgery, dental care, ambulance services or illness arising en route to Australia. The agreements do not cover repatriation in the case of illness or injury.

You are allowed to bring 'reasonable quantities' of prescribed, non-narcotic medications. All should be clearly labelled and identifiable. For large quantities, bring a doctor's certificate to produce to Customs if necessary. All medication must be carried in personal hand luggage. Local chemists can fill most prescriptions – which must be written by an Australian-registered doctor.

Health hazards exist on the seas and in the countryside, starting with the threat of too much sun. High-factor sun-screen cream is essential if exposed, even on cloudy days.

Poisonous spiders live in Australia. The dark, bulbous, Sydney funnelweb is one of the world's most lethal and aggressive types of spider. Although its bites are rare (about 10 victims a year), they require immediate medical attention to stave off coma and death. Catch the spider for identification if you can. Other poisonous spiders include the redback, the eastern mouse spider and the white-tail.

Shark attacks are also rare, but one is too many and may well be your last. In 2000, sharks killed more people in Australia than anywhere else. (Before you get too alarmed, the death toll was three – out of seven attacks in Australian waters.) Swim between the flags and heed shark alarms.

In certain seasons and areas, bluebottles and other dangerous **jellyfish** may be encountered. Their sting is agonising but can be treated. Never disregard warning signs on beaches. In the north of Australia, **saltwater crocodiles** can be a menace to swimmers. Again, obey the signs. Other marine hazards include the camouflaged stonefish and the blue-ringed octopus. Both can cause convulsions, paralysis and death. Several of the world's deadliest **snakes**, including the brown snake, tiger snake, taipan and death adder, are indigenous to Australia. You are unlikely to encounter them in built-up areas. The inland taipan, or fierce snake, has the most potent venom in the world, but is restricted to sparsely populated areas of southwest Queensland, so few people are bitten. If you are bitten by any snake, seek immediate medical attention.

The good news is that you can drink water from taps anywhere unless specifically marked otherwise. In the Outback, warnings may read 'Bore water' or 'Not for drinking'.

HITCH-HIKING

It's better not to hitch-hike, which is banned on freeways and throughout the whole state of Queensland. Even where it is tolerated, it can be risky. Some city hostels feature notice boards where people driving interstate can advertise for a travelling companion to share costs. That way, you at least get to meet the person you might travel with. Cut-rate bus travel is a safer and better option.

HOLIDAYS

1 January	New Year's Day
26 January	Australia Day
25 April	Anzac Day
25 December	Christmas Day
26 December	Boxing Day
Moveable dates	Good Friday, Easter, Easter Monday, Queen's Birthday

Certain other public holidays are celebrated only in certain states, while other holidays are observed at different times in different states. School holidays arrive four times a year; the longest one is in the summer through the latter part of December and all of January, tending to crowd hotels and tourist attractions.

L

LANGUAGE

Australian is spoken everywhere – that is to say, English with a distinctive accent. The vernacular is sometimes called 'Strine', which is the way the word 'Australian' sounds in an extreme Australian pronunciation. While educated and cultivated Australians tend to speak in more neutral accents, Strine in the backblocks can sound to an American ear like a profound Cockney intonation piped through the nose, while British visitors ('Poms') may detect an American influence. Here are a few Australian terms and colloquialisms:

across the ditch	over the Tasman Sea, ie New Zealand
ankle-biter	young child
arvo	afternoon
back of Bourke	far Outback
banana bender	Queenslander
beaut	(from beautiful) very good, fantastic
billabong	waterhole in a semi-dry river
bitser	mongrel (bits of this and bits of that)
bludger	sponger, tightwad
bonzer	terrific
boomer	huge kangaroo
bunyip	Australia's yeti or Bigfoot
cask	box of cheap wine
chook	chicken
cossie	swimming costume
crook	broken, sick, no good
dag	mild term for fool or uncool person; the popular adjective is **daggy**
damper	unleavened bread, usually cooked in a camp fire, a staple of bush tucker
dinkie die	the truth
dinkum	genuine or honest
drongo	idiot

dunny	toilet ('As useless as a glass door on a dunny')
esky	cooler
galah	fool (after the parrot of the same name)
greenie	conservationist
grizzle	complain
heart starter	first drink of the day
hoon	loudmouth
jackaroo	male worker on an outback station
jillaroo	female ditto
jumbuck	lamb
kark it	to die
lob	arrive ('to lob in')
lurk	racket or illegal scheme
middy	285ml/10oz glass of beer (in NSW)
neck oil	beer
nervy	nervous attack ('to chuck a nervy')
ocker	bumpkin, loudmouth
pokie	slot machine
ripper	very good
roo	kangaroo
root	have sexual intercourse
rooted	exhausted
scunge	dirty, untidy person
she'll be apples	it'll be fine
shoot through	leave unexpectedly, escape
snags	sausages
stickybeak	busybody
strain the potatoes	urinate
stubby	small bottle of beer
tinnie or **tube**	can of beer
Top End	north part of Northern Territory
ute	pick-up (utility) truck
wowser	kiljoy, prude
yabber	chatter
yakka	work

LAUNDRY AND DRY CLEANING

Hotels and motels usually offer one-day laundry and dry cleaning service for guests, but it can be quite expensive. Ask the receptionist, porter or maid. Many hotels and motels also have launderette facilities on the premises.

M

MAPS

State and local tourist offices give away useful maps of their areas. If you need more detailed maps, check at newsstands and bookshops. Car hire companies often supply free city directories showing each street and place of interest. If you're driving beyond the cities you'll want to buy an up-to-date road map of the region.

MEDIA

More than 500 newspapers are published in Australia, ranging from internationally esteemed big-city dailies like the *Sydney Morning Herald* and *The Age* of Melbourne to numerous backwoods weeklies. Among the latter are local periodicals aimed at the various immigrant communities, published in Dutch, French, German, Greek, Italian and other languages. In the bigger cities, specialist newsstands provide airmail copies of newspapers from London, Rome, New York and Paris, in addition to weekly and monthly American and European magazines.

CNN and other satellite news services are available at most international-standard hotels, and you may be able to read your hometown paper on the Internet at one of the many Internet cafés around Australia.

MONEY

You don't have to reach for a credit card to use plastic in Australia – banknotes are made of it and feature transparent panels instead of watermarks. Australian currency is decimal, with the dollar the basic unit (100 cents to one dollar). Notes come in A\$100, A\$50, A\$20, A\$10 and A\$5 denominations. Coins come in 5c, 10c, 20c, 50c, A\$1 and A\$2 denominations. One quirk persists – it's still legal for shops to express prices in coins that no longer circulate. If something is priced at A\$11.99, it will cost you A\$12.

As for **credit cards**, American Express, Bankcard, MasterCard, Visa and Diners Club are widely accepted, but you may have problems with them in smaller towns and country areas and small retail shops.

All international airports in Australia provide **currency exchange** facilities, and foreign notes or travellers' cheques can be converted at most banks. Cash travellers' cheques at banks or larger hotels (despite the charges), as it may be difficult elsewhere. Know that Australian banks charge for just about everything these days.

ATM **cards** are widely used and machines are widespread. You should be able to obtain cash directly in this way using the same PIN number you use at home.

N

NATIONAL PARKS

Information on the country's national parks can be obtained from the **Australian Nature Conservation Agency**, GPO Box 787, Canberra, ACT 2601; tel: (02) 6274 1111; <www.ea.gov.au>, or from the offices managing each region:

New South Wales: National Parks and Wildlife Service, 110 George Street, Sydney, NSW 2000; tel: (02) 02 9253 4600; <www.npws. nsw.gov.au>.

Australian Capital Territory: ACT Parks and Conservation Service, GPO Box 1065, Tuggeranong, ACT 2901; tel: (02) 6237 5222;

Queensland: Queensland Parks and Wildlife Service, GPO Box 155, Albert Street, Brisbane, Queensland 4002; Tel: (07) 3227 8186; <www.epa.qld.gov.au/environment/park>.

Northern Territory: Parks and Wildlife Commission of Northern Territory, Goyder Centre, 25 Chung Wah Terrace, Palmerston, NT 0830; tel: (08) 8999 5511; <www.nt.gov.au/ipe/paw>.

Western Australia: Conservation and Land Management (CALM), Hackett Drive, Crawley, WA 6009; tel: (08) 9442 0300; <www.calm. wa.gov.au>.

South Australia: National Parks and Wildlife Service, GPO Box 1047, Adelaide, SA 5001; tel: (08) 8204 1910; <www.environment.sa. gov.au/parks>.

Victoria: Parks Victoria, Level 10, 535 Bourke Street, Melbourne, Victoria 3000; tel: (03) 8627 4699; <www.parkweb.vic.gov.au>.

Tasmania: National Parks and Wildlife Service, 134 Macquarie Street Hobart, Tasmania 7000; tel: (03) 6233 6191; <www.dpiwe.tas. gov.au>.

O

OPENING HOURS

Banks generally open from 9.30am to 4pm Monday to Thursday and from 9.30am to 5pm on Fridays. In big cities, selected banking facilities may be available on Saturday morning, but don't rely on it.

General **office hours** are 9am to 5pm, Monday to Friday, and **post offices** follow the same hours. Stamps are often available at the front desks of hotels and motels and at some retail outlets.

Shopping: Most shops close at 5 or 5.30pm on weekdays. In most towns, shops have one (or sometimes two) late shopping nights a week, when stores stay open to 9 or 9.30 pm. This is usually on Thursday or Friday. Sunday trading is becoming more common in larger cities, and some stores operate 24 hours a day.

Bars/pubs/hotels: Licensing hours vary by state, but a typical schedule would be 10am–10pm Monday to Saturday, with most pubs open by noon on Sundays as well.

P

POLICE

Each state operates its own police force, covering both urban and rural areas. The federal police force has jurisdiction over government property, including airports.

The police emergency telephone number is 000.

POST OFFICES

Australia's post offices are signposted 'Australia Post'. Most branches adhere to a 9am–5pm schedule Monday to Friday, though big-city General Post Offices often remain open for extended hours.

Postcards cost 95 cents to the US and A$1 to Europe. Letters cost A$1.05 and A$1.20 respectively, and international aerograms cost 70 cents, whatever their destination. Mailboxes throughout Australia are red, with an Australia Post logo. Most post offices have fax facilities, as do hotels. Internet cafés exist in all Australian cities and are spreading rapidly in small centres, too.

PUBLIC TRANSPORT

This is highly developed in most Australian cities, with buses and trains being the most frequent form. Sydney Airport is now connected directly to the city by rail.

Sydney has its quirky monorail that links the central city to Darling Harbour, and also has a light rail system from Central Station to Chinatown, the Fish Markets and beyond. A fine fleet of ferries, sailing 6am–11pm daily, are concentrated at Circular Quay. The ferries provide cheap outings for sightseers to Kirribilli, Neutral Bay or Taronga Zoo.

Melbourne's trams are not only decorative – they're a vital part of city transport. The gold-and-burgundy-coloured City Circle tram is free. In Adelaide, trams run to Glenelg, and the O-bahn ('bullet bus') provides highly efficient transport.

R

RELIGION

The major religion in Australia is Christianity. In the late 1990s, the numbers of Roman Catholics overtook the number of Anglicans (Church of England). Next in line, numerically, are the Uniting Church, Presbyterian and Orthodox. Of the non-Christian faiths, Muslims are the largest group, followed by Jews and Buddhists. To find the church of your choice, check at your hotel desk or look in the Yellow Pages of the telephone directory under 'Churches and Synagogues'. Most of the major religions will be represented.

T

TELEPHONES

Australia's country code is 61. This is followed by a city code, generally 2 for NSW or the ATC, 3 for Victoria and Tasmania, 7 for Queensland and 8 for the Northern Territory, South Australia or Western Australia.

Australia's telephone network is sophisticated; you can dial anywhere in the country from almost any phone, even in the Outback, and expect a loud and clear line. Many hotel rooms have phones from which you can dial cross-Australia (STD) or internationally (IDD). Some hotels add a surcharge to your telephone bill.

The minimum cost of a local public payphone call is 40c. Long-distance calls within Australia (STD) and International Direct Dialing (IDD) calls can be made on Telstra public payphones. Check with the operator for these charges as they vary for distances and the time of day of the call. Public payphones accept most coins and Phonecards. A Phonecard is a pre-paid card for use in public payphones to make local, STD and IDD calls. Phonecards are widely sold at newsstands and other shops, and come in denominations of A$5, A$10, A$20 and A$50. The Telstra PhoneAway pre-paid card enables you to use virtually any phone in Australia – home and office phones, mobile phones, hotel and payphones – all call costs are charged against the card. If you need assistance, help is available in seven languages.

Creditphones accept most major credit cards such as Amex, Visa and MasterCard and can be found at international and domestic airports, central-city locations and many hotels. Country Direct is a service that lets you speak directly with an operator in your home country or you can use an automated service. Cash is not needed as the call is charged to the receiving number or to your telephone credit card. Country Direct calling guides are available through Telstra shops, travel agents and tour operators.

Telephone directories give full instructions on dialling and details on emergency and other services. To reach an overseas number, dial 0011, then the country code of the destination, the area code and the local number.

TIME ZONES

Australia has three distinct time zones: Australian Eastern Standard Time (EST), which operates in New South Wales, Australian Capital Territory, Victoria, Tasmania and Queensland; Central Standard Time (CST) in South Australia and Northern Territory (and in the NSW Outback town of Broken Hill); and Western Standard Time (WST) in Western Australia.

CST is 30 minutes behind EST, while WST is two hours behind EST. Daylight saving (setting the clocks forward an hour) operates in New South Wales, Australian Capital Territory (Canberra and surrounds), Victoria and South Australia from the end of October through to the end of March, and in Tasmania from the beginning of October to the end of March. The Northern Territory, Western Australia and Queensland do not apply daylight saving during the summer.

Sydney is on EST, which is 10 hours ahead of Greenwich Mean Time and 15 hours ahead of New York. Time differences between Australia's zones and other countries vary seasonally as daylight saving is switched on and off by Australia or the other country. So when it's winter in the northern hemisphere, and daylight saving is operating in New South Wales, the time difference between London and Sydney is 11 hours. But during British Summertime, when Sydney is on EST, it's only nine hours. One way to get it right is to access <www.whitepages.com.au> on the Internet and use the time zone calculator.

TIPPING

Tipping is discretionary and a relatively recent custom. Nobody's livelihood depends on tipping. It is not customary to tip taxi drivers, porters at airports or hairdressers, although you may do so if you wish. Porters have set charges at railway terminals, but not at hotels. Hotels and restaurants do not add service charges to accounts. In better-class restaurants, patrons sometimes tip food and drink waiters up to 10 percent, but only if service is good. (If you are ecstatic about the service, make it 15 percent.) Tipping is what it should be – an optional gratuity for good service. It has not developed into a means of subsidising wages. If service is poor or a waiter is surly or impolite, don't tip.

TOILETS

Australians manage without euphemisms for 'toilet', though in a country so rich in slang you won't be surprised to come across some wry synonyms. 'Dunny' is the Outback slang term, but 'washroom', 'restrooms', 'ladies' or 'gents' are all understood. Toilets are often locked after certain hours, but you can generally use the facilities in any pub or cinema complex without needing to buy a drink or a movie ticket. Toilets are generally clean, even in the Outback. While on that subject, it's wise to check under Outback toilet seats to ensure no poisonous redback spider is lurking there. They like that location.

TOURIST INFORMATION

To obtain tourist information before you leave home, access the comprehensive web site of the Australian Tourist Commission (ATC)

<www.austalia.com> or contact them in your country of residence or at their Australian head office: Level 4, 80 William Street, Woolloomooloo, Sydney, NSW 2011, Australia; tel: 1300 361 650.

Overseas ATC offices are:

United Kingdom: Gemini House, 10-18 Putney Hill, Putney, London SW15 6AA; tel: (020) 8780 2229; fax: (020) 8780 1496.

USA: 2049 Century Park East, Suite 1920, Los Angeles CA, 90067; tel: (310) 229 4870; fax: (310) 552 1215.

New Zealand: Level 13, 44-48 Emily Place, Auckland 1; tel: (09) 379 9594; fax: (09) 307 3117.

Japan: c/o Australian Business Centre, New Otani Garden Court Building, 28F 4-1, Kioi-cho, Chiyoda-Ku Tokyo, 102 Japan; tel: (03) 5214 0720; fax: (03) 5214 0719.

Hong Kong: Central Plaza, Suite 1501, 18 Harbour Road, Wanchai; tel: (852) 2802 7700; fax: (852) 2802 8211.

Korea: Suite 801, Hotel President 188-3, Ulchiro 1-ka, Chung-ku, Seoul 100-191 Korea; tel: (81-3) 5214 0720; fax: (81-3) 5214 0719.

Singapore: #26-05 United Square, 101 Thomson Road, Singapore 307591; tel: (65) 255 4555; fax: (65) 253 8431.

Once in Australia, even in the smallest town you will find an outlet distributing local tourist information and advice free of charge. Look for the international 'i' sign.

W

WEB SITES

Australian Tourist Commission: <www.australia.com>
Travel Online: <www.travelonline.com>
Travel Australia: <http://www.atn.com.au>
Western Australian Tourism Commission: <www.westernaustralia.net>
Northern Territory Tourist Commission: <www.nttc.com.au>
Tourism Tasmania: <www.tourism.tas.gov.au>

Tourism Victoria: <www.tourismvictoria.com.au>
Tourism New South Wales: <www.tourism.nsw.gov.au>
South Australian Tourist Commission: <www.southaustralia.com>
Tourism Queensland: <www.queensland-holidays.com.au>
Canberra Tourism: <www.canberratourism.com.au>
Visas: <www.immi.gov.au>
Latest currency exchange rates: <www.xe.net>
Australian Government: <www.fed.gov.au>
Sydney Morning Herald: <www.smh.com.au>
Melbourne Age: <www.theage.com.au>

WEIGHTS AND MEASURES

Since the 1960s, Australia has moved to the metric system. Old-timers may still refer to distances in miles, and some inner-city, mock-Irish pubs persist in selling beer by the pint, but generally the abandonment of British Imperial measures has taken total effect.

Y

YOUTH HOSTELS

There are two types of hostel accommodation: privately-owned back-packer hostels and YHA (Youth Hostels Association) Hostels. Both provide self-catering accommodation from about A\$20 a night.

The Australian YHA is Australia's largest budget accommodation network, running more than 130 hostels in just about every place you might want to go in Australia. 'Youth' is a relative term, for the hostels are open to all ages and offer sleeping, self-catering kitchens and common rooms where you'll meet fellow travellers.

You can join the YHA in your own country or in Australia. Contact the YHA (422 Kent Street, Sydney, NSW 2001; tel: (02) 9261 1111; <www.yha.com.au>) for a free information pack giving membership details and a list of hostels.

INDEX